Kafir Stories

William Charles Scully

ESPRIOS.COM
ESPRIOS DIGITAL PUBLISHING

KAFIR STORIES
SEVEN SHORT STORIES

BY

WILLIAM CHARLES SCULLY

AUTHOR OF

"POEMS, " ETC., ETC.

1895

TO

KATE FREILIGRATH KROEKER

AND

J. H. MEIRING BECK THIS BOOK IS INSCRIBED.

"So geographers, in Afric maps,
With savage pictures fill their gaps,
And o'er uninhabitable downs
Place elephants for want of towns."

SWIFT.

CONTENTS

I. THE EUMENIDES IN KAFIRLAND

II. THE FUNDAMENTAL AXIOM

III. KELLSON'S NEMESIS

IV. THE QUEST OF THE COPPER

V. GHAMBA

VI. UKUSHWAMA

VII. UMTAGATI

Glossary

Allemagtig, almighty

Boomslang, an innocuous colubrine snake

*Donga, a gully with steep sides

Drift, the ford of a river

*E-hea, exactly so

*Ewe, yes

Hamel, a wether sheep

*Icanti, a fabulous serpent, the mere appearance of which is supposed to cause death

*Impandulu, the lightning bird. The Kafirs believe the lightning to be a bird

*Impi, an army or any military force on the war path

*Induna, a Zulu councilor or general

Kapater, a wether goat

Kerrie, a stick such as is almost invariably carried by a Kafir

Kloof, a gorge or valley

Kaffirboom, a large arboreal aloe

Kopje, an abrupt hillock

Kraal, (1) an enclosure for stock; a fold or pen. (2) a native hut, or collection of huts

Krantz, a cliff

*Lobola, the payment of cattle by a man to the father of the girl he

wants to marry

*Mawo, an exclamation of surprise

Mealies, maize

Op togt, on a trading trip

Ou Pa, grandfather

Outspan, to unyoke a team

Raak, hit

Reim, a leather thong

Reimje, diminutive of foregoing

Schulpad, a tortoise

Sjambok: a heavy whip made of rhinocerous hide

Stoep, a space about two yards, in width along the front or side of a house. Usually covered by a verandah in the case of South African houses

Taaibosch, "tough bush," a shrub. Rhus lucida

*Tikoloshe, a water spirit who is supposed, when people are drowned, to have pulled them under water by the feet

"Ukushwama, the feast of first fruits;—celebrated by the Bacas and some other Bantu tribes

*Umtagati, magic;—witchcraft

Veldt. unenclosed and uncultivated land. The open country

Veldschoens, home-made boots such as those in general use amongst South African Boers

Voor-huis, the dining and sitting-room in a Dutch house

*Yebo, yes

*Kafir terms are marked by an asterisk.

THE EUMENIDES IN KAFIRLAND.

"Fate leadeth through the garden shews
The trees of Knowledge, Death, and Life;
On this, the wholesome apple grows,—
On that, fair fruit with poison rife.
Yet sometimes apples deadly be.
Whilst poison-fruits may nourish thee."

SHAGBAG'S Advice to Beginners.

I.

THIS is how it all happened. They met at the canteen on Monday morning at eight o'clock—Jim Gubo, the policeman, and Kalaza, who had just been released from the convict station where, for five long years, he had been expiating a particularly cruel assault with violence upon a woman. 'Ntsoba, the fat Fingo barman, leant lazily over the counter, but as the regular customers for the morning "nip" had all departed, and no one else had yet come, he went outside and sat in the sunshine, smoking his oily pipe with thorough enjoyment. He did not in the least mind leaving Jim Gubo in the canteen, because Jim and he had long since come to an understanding, and this with the full approval of the proprietor. Jim was, so to say, free of the house, and got his daily number of tots of poisonous "dop" brandy measured out in the thick glass tumbler, the massive exterior of which was quite out of proportion to the comparatively limited interior space. These tots (and an occasional bottle) were Jim's reward for not exercising too severe a supervision over the canteen, and for always happening to be round the corner when a row took place. Moreover, the till, besides being as yet nearly empty, was well out of reach; the counter was high and broad, and the shelving, sparsely filled with filthy looking black bottles, was fixed well back, so as to be out of the way of the whirling kerries which were often in evidence, especially on Saturday afternoons. The great brown, poisonous looking hogsheads—suggestive of those very much swollen and unpleasant looking fecund female insects which are to be found in the nethermost chamber of the city of the termites, and which lay thousands of eggs daily—had safety taps, of which 'Ntsoba's master kept the keys.

Kafir Stories

Jim Gubo and Kalaza talked about many things—of life at the convict station, for Kalaza was the nephew of Jim's father's second wife, and Jim consequently knew all about his companion; of the decadence of the times, in which it was so difficult for a poor man to live without working; of the strictness with which the locations were managed; of how the inspectors inquired inconveniently as to strangers therein sojourning, and chiefly about the decline in Jim's particular line of business.

"Son of my father, " said Jim, "times are very bad indeed. There is little or no stock-stealing going on. The farmers come to the office and report losses of sheep; we are sent to hunt for the thieves, but instead of catching them, we find that the sheep have simply strayed into some other farmer's flock. Will you believe it; for two months we have not run in a single thief? "

"Mawo, " replied Kalaza, "how very discouraging. "

"Yes, and Government thinks we are not doing our duty, and my officer says we are no good. "

"But can you not make them steal, or make the magistrate think they do? " rejoined Kalaza, after a pause.

"Wait a bit, that is what I am coming to, " said Jim, in a low tone. "There is one man whom I know to be a thief, but though I have tried to, over and over again, I cannot catch him. "

"Who is that? "

"Maliwe, the son of Zangalele, the Kafir whose brother Tambiso gave evidence against you when you were tried by the judge. "

Here the beady eyes of Kalaza gave a kind of snap, and he leant forward with an appearance of increased interest.

"Tell me about Maliwe, " he said.

"Maliwe, " replied Jim, "is the shepherd of Gert Botha, whose farm is near the Gangili Hill, where the two rivers join. "

Kalaza pondered for a few seconds, and then asked:

"But what makes you think he steals? "

"Well, you know what a Kafir is. Maliwe lives alongside the sheep, in a hut on the mountain—all alone. The kraal is far from the homestead. Gert Botha never gives his servants enough to eat, and Maliwe must often be hungry. There you have it—a man hungry night after night, and close to him a kraal fall of fat sheep. You know!"

"Does Maliwe ever go to beer-drinks? "

"Not often, for being a Kafir, the Fingoes would most likely beat him to death. No, he lives quietly and to himself. He has been in Botha's service since just after he was circumcised, three years ago. He gets a cow every year as wages, and each cow as he receives it is given to old Dalisile, who lives on another part of Botha's farm, and whose daughter Maliwe is paying lobola for. They say he means to earn two more cows and then to marry the girl. But I fear he is hopeless. "

Kalaza again pondered, his beady eyes twinkling incessantly.

"Do you ever employ detectives now? " he asked.

"Oh, yes, " said Jim lightly, "we do so now and then. But he that is hired must prove that duty has been done before he gets paid. "

"How so? "

"By making some one guilty, and causing him to be sentenced by the magistrate. When he has done this, the detective gets fifteen shillings. Well, I must go to the camp. Have a drink? "

'Ntsoba came lazily in at Jim's call, and handed him a tot. This Jim took into his mouth. He rolled it round his gums, he wagged his tongue in it. He let it flow far back into his throat, and then brought it forward again. Kalaza came and stood before him, and opened his mouth wide. Into this, Jim deliberately, and with an aim so sure that not a drop was lost, squirted about half the tot. Kalaza thereupon wagged his tongue, rolled the liquor round ins gums, and then swallowed it slowly.

At the door of the canteen they parted.

"Good-bye, son of my father," said Kalaza.

"Yes, my friend," replied Jim, and walked away slowly towards the police camp.

Kalaza shouldered his stick and went off quickly in the direction of the native location.

II.

Maliwe drove home his flock at sunset, and penned them safely in the kraal, which was constructed of heavy thorn bushes. The old kapater goat, which acted as bellwether of the flock, strode proudly into the enclosure, well ahead of the others, and took his station on a rock which rose up in the middle. On this he lay down, chewing his cud and surveying the sheep which lay thickly around him. Maliwe then closed the gate, tied it securely with a reim, and pulled several large bushes against it. He then walked on to his little hut, situated only a few yards distant. He had carried in from the veldt a small number of dry sticks, and he now placed a few of the smallest of these in a little heap on the raised stone which served as fireplace. He then drew out his tinder-box from the leather bag which he always carried. This bag was simply the skin of a kid, the head of which had been cut off, and the body drawn out through the aperture at the neck thus made. He struck a spark with his flint, and when the tinder glowed, he shook out a little of it on to some dry grass, which soon blazed up, and which he then placed under the twigs. In a few minutes he had a cheerful fire, and then he untied his little three-legged pot from where it hung from one of the wattles of the roof. This pot was half full of mealies already cooked, and which he simply meant to warm for his supper. The remainder of his week's ration of meat (the skinny ribs of a goat that had died of debility down near his master's homestead) was also hanging from the roof, but with a sigh he determined to reserve that delicacy for the morrow, remembering that two days would elapse before a fresh supply was due. His dog, Sibi—a starved looking mongrel greyhound—lay at his feet and gazed up with expectant eyes, waiting for the handful of tough mealies which would be flung to him when his master had finished supper.

It was a clear starlit night in Spring. Supper over, Maliwe sat on the ground just outside the floor of the hut, and thought of Nalai, the daughter of old Dalisile, for whom he was paying lobola. In a month more, another year's service would be completed, and another cow would be his. This he meant to take as he had taken the two already earned, and deliver to his prospective father-in-law. His mother had promised him the calf of her only cow as soon as it should be weaned, and then he hoped that old Dalisile, skinflint as he was, would deliver the girl, trusting him for payment of the fifth and last beast in course of time. In two or, at the outside, three months this calf would be weaned. It was a red bull with white face and feet—he knew every mark, and one might almost say every hair on the animal, having looked at it so often. It was a remarkably fine calf, but Maliwe thought it took a strangely long time in growing up. He lit his pipe, and dreamt dreams. Soon he would be no longer alone in his hut. He loved the girl Nalai, and she seemed to love him, so the future was bright. She was tall and straight, still unbent by that toil which is the portion of the female Kafir. Her teeth gleamed very white, and her breast swelled each year more temptingly over the edge other red blanket. As boy and girl they had grown up together, and long before she was of a marriageable age, he had determined eventually to marry her. So he went away and worked for three long years; his strong, self-contained nature needing nothing but this one fixed idea to steady it. Maliwe was not what is known as a "School Kafir. " He was quite uncivilised in every respect, and was utterly heathen. He could speak no word of any language except his own, and he believed implicitly in "Tikoloshe" and the "Lightning Bird. "

His pipe finished, Maliwe arose and fetched a musical instrument from the hut. This consisted of a stick about three feet long, bent into a bow by a string made of twisted sinews. About eight inches from one end was fixed a small dry gourd, with a hole large enough, to admit a five shilling piece cut out of the side furthest from the point of attachment. Music is made on such an instrument by holding it so that that part of the gourd where the aperture is, is pressed against the naked breast, and then twanging on the string with a small stick. About four notes can be extracted by a skilful player. The result is not cheerful, and to the civilised ear the strains of a Jew's harp are preferable. But the twanging eased the burthen of longing which Maliwe bore, and no lute-player in passionate Andalusia ever poured out his love in melody with more genuine feeling than did this savage on his "U-hade. "

Maliwe had waited through these long years—and how long are not the years under such circumstances? —with a kind of contented impatience, and as time went by, the impatience waxed and the contentment waned. With the premonition of genuine love he had seen the budding woman of today in the child of three years ago. He had worked and waited. His reward was now near, and anticipation was sweet. In imagination he saw the little brown babies with the weasel-tooth necklets, tumbling about the hut and toddling up the path to meet him when he drove home his nock in the evening, whilst Nalai stood at the door looking with pride on their progeny.

Sibi, the dog, gave a low growl, and then rushed along the footpath barking furiously. A man emerged from the darkness, keeping the dog at bay with his kerrie. Maliwe, seeing nothing suspicious about the stranger, called off the dog, which retired still growling into the hut. The man approached.

"Greeting, Maliwe, " he cried. "Do you not know me? "

"Greeting, " replied Maliwe, "but I do not know you. Where are you thinking of? " [A native idiom. It means "Where are you going to? "]

"Hear him, " cried the visitor. "He does not know me. He does not know Kalaza, the only Fingo his father Zangalele ever made a friend of. He does not know the man who used to cut sticks for him when he was a little boy. "

"Sit down, Kalaza, " replied Maliwe, "I meant no offence. I do not remember you, but if you were my father's friend, you are mine. "

So they went into the hut, and they refreshed the fire, and they talked, and they put some dry mealies to roast with fat in the three-legged pot, and they talked of Maliwe's relations, of old Dalisile, and of his daughter Nalai whom Maliwe was going to marry.

Kalaza said that he lived in Kwala's location beyond the Keiskamma, that he was a very rich man with a large herd of cattle, and that he was now seeking two cows lately received as lobola for one of his daughters from a man in the Albany district, and which were supposed to have strayed homewards. He also said, that although a Fingo, he always preferred the society of Kafirs, and that for this reason he had come to spend the night with Maliwe instead of with the Fingoes in the village location.

By and by the mealies began to "pop" in the pot, so guest and host began to chew them. "It is sad to be old and have such bad teeth, " said Kalaza, as he paused in his chewing. "Have you not got a little meat? "

Maliwe stood up, and reaching to the roof of the hut, handed down the emaciated ribs of the goat. Kalaza took the meat, turned it over critically, and handed it back.

"That is the meat of an old, tough goat, " he said, "I could no more chew that than the mealies. "

"I am very sorry, " replied Maliwe, "but I have none other. "

At this Kalaza sighed, said he was an old man, and he supposed times had changed since he was young, but in his day no old man would be so treated by the son of his best friend. Maliwe remained silent for some time, and then said politely that he was a servant, and had to be content with what food his master gave him. Breaking up some tobacco in his hand, he reached it over to Kalaza, asking if he cared, to smoke. Kalaza refused the offer, saying that since becoming old he had been unable to enjoy tobacco on an empty stomach. He then sighed heavily, and sat looking at the fire until the silence became oppressive.

By and by Maliwe asked if he would not go to sleep, and then Kalaza began to wax indignant.

"You call yourself a man, " he said, "and you let your father's best friend die of hunger. Did I not know you had been circumcised, I should think you were still a boy. "

"Friend of my father, " replied Maliwe, "I have given you all I have. Do you want to eat my dog? "

"Given me all you have? What are those animals that I hear bleating outside? "

"My master's sheep. "

"Your master's sheep? Ho! ho! When hungry men are about, sheep have no master. Would your father have let me die rather than take a hamel from the flock of a rich, lazy boer, who never counts his sheep. Many a sheep your father and I have lifted in the old days. We never wanted meat. If my son were to let your father hunger, I would break his head. "

In the foregoing remarks the tempter had accidentally hit upon a fact. Gert Botha, after a three years' experience of Maliwe's honesty and carefulness, very seldom took the trouble to count his sheep.

"Friend of my father, " said Maliwe, "I have never yet taken what belonged to another. If you say my father stole, it may be so—but such must have happened when he was young. He is now dead. When I was a lad he told me he would kill me if I stole. "

"Just as you say, when he was young, " rejoined Kalaza. "And are you, then, old? I wonder does old Dalisile know what a coward he is giving his daughter to. In the good old days he would have sent you to show that you could steal like a man—a young man—before you got your wife. But it does not matter, I shall not die tonight, although I am old. "

All this time Maliwe sat looking fixedly at the speaker, who, after a pause, continued:

"My son Tentu wants a wife. I will go to Dalisile tomorrow and see whether seven fat oxen will not tempt him to return your three skinny cows, and send his daughter to my kraal across to Keiskamma, I have heard of Nalai, and I think she will suit Tentu; at my kraal she will never want milk. "

Here again chance favoured the tempter. The one dread of Maliwe's life was the rivalry of a rich suitor.

Maliwe bent his head over his knees, and remained in this posture for a few minutes. He then stood up suddenly and strode out of the hut. Just afterwards a sound as of sheep rushing about might have been heard coming from the direction of the kraal. Kalaza heard it, and smiled. A few minutes elapsed, and then Maliwe returned, carrying a young sheep with its throat cut on his shoulder. This he flung down on to the ground before Kalaza, saying:

"Friend of my father, here is meat. Eat! "

Maliwe then seized his stick, called Sibi the dog, and left the hut. Kalaza skinned the sheep, and eat about a third of the meat, selecting the choicest parts. He then buried the remainder of the carcase, with the skin, in the loose, dry dung at the side of the kraal. Having done this he walked off quickly in the direction of the village.

After leaving the hut, Maliwe climbed a rocky ridge, which rose steeply for about a hundred yards at the back of the kraal. On the comb of the ridge stood an immense boulder, and Maliwe spent the rest of the night sitting to lee-ward of this, Sibi, the dog, curled up at his feet, growling at intervals, and every now and then looking in the direction of the hut, which was, like the kraal, out of sight, with cars cocked and nostrils dilated.

III.

Just before dawn, Maliwe suddenly fell into the deep sleep of nervous exhaustion. His knees were drawn up, and his head, bent forward, rested on them sideways, He was still asleep when the sun arose and warmed his chilled limbs. He was wakened suddenly by the loud barking of the dog, so he bounded to his feet and ran round the boulder, to a spot from whence he could see the hut and the kraal. Some people on horseback had just reached the hut, and one dismounted and looked in. He recognized them all. There was his master, Gert Botha, on his old grey mare; there was the European sergeant, of the Cape Police; there was private Jim Gubo of the same force, and there was Kalaza, the "friend of his father" and his guest of the previous night.

As he stood looking, some one called out, "There he is! " The wretched man then realised his situation. His first impulse was to fly—all the savage in him prompting towards an escape into the bush, which lay temptingly near. He sprang back and ran—fleet as a bush-buck towards the cover. But after running a few yards he stopped dead still, and then, turning round, walked slowly back over the ridge in the direction of the hut. As he crossed the comb, he was met by the sergeant and Jim Gubo, breathless from running up the steep hill. By them he was promptly hand-cuffed, and then led down to where his master was standing, between the hut and the kraal. The old goat was walking up and down inside the kraal gate, tinkling his bell and wondering why he and his flock had not been let out at the usual time. Kalaza pointed out to Gert Botha the blood stains which were to be seen plentifully distributed over the floor and poles of the hut, and then walked round the kraal. When he reached a certain spot he paused, and began probing in the loose dung with his stick. He then called out to Jim Gubo, who joined him, and the skin and other remains of the slaughtered animal were soon brought to light.

Maliwe, when confronted with his master, looked him straight in the face. Gert Botha lifted the heavy sjambok which he usually carried, and struck the prisoner heavily over the bare head and face. A thick, grey wheal immediately followed the blow, but Maliwe did not even wince. "Jou verdomde parmantig schepsel, " cried the irate Boer. "Ik neuk jou uit jou hartnakigheid. " (You infernal, insolent fellow, I will have you out of your stiff-neckedness.) Botha would have struck him again, had not the sergeant interfered.

So Maliwe was marched, carrying the corpus delicti, in to the gaol. Within an hour after his arrival, the magistrate sentenced him to receive twenty-live lashes with a cat o' nine tails on the bare back, and to pay a fine of five pounds, being five times the value of the slaughtered sheep according to Gert Botha's computation. In levying the fine, the two cows which he had given as lobola were seized — much against the will of old Dalisile. Out of the proceeds, Gert Botha was paid the value of the sheep, and Kalaza received fifteen shillings, which he, in company with Jim Gubo, spent the same day at the canteen.

Sibi, the dog, hung about the gaol howling, until he was driven away with stones. He then returned to his master's hut, and howled there all the afternoon and through the night. Next morning, Gert Botha's son Andries shot him.

Maliwe received his twenty-five lashes, and was discharged from prison, after his back had, under the superintendence of the District Surgeon, been well washed with brine, to prevent evil results. Neither under the flogging nor the pickling did Maliwe exhibit the slightest sign of the torture which he suffered.

On the same evening Maliwe went to a certain tree, just at the back of old Dalisile's huts, and gave a long, low whistle, which was the established signal between himself and Nalai. Unfortunately, however, Nalai did not hear him, but her two big brothers, Kawana and Joli, did. Old Dalisile, anticipating Maliwe's visit, had kept Nalai out of the way, and put his two sons to watch. These fell upon Maliwe and smote him so hard with their kerries, that he lay for a long time senseless on the ground. When he regained consciousness, he limped quietly away.

He has not since been heard of in the neighbourhood.

Kafir Stories

THE FUNDAMENTAL AXIOM.

The wild ass of the desert knows,
By inborn knowledge, friends from foes.
The tame ass of the village browses
Contentedly between the houses.
He has no foes, he has no friends,
He toils and eats until he ends.

But this time, Fate, on grim jokes bent,
A wild ass to the village sent.
Oh, what a tempest shook the village,
'Twas worse than flood, or fire, or pillage!

Now if an ass I needs must be,
The desert's joys and pains for me

Broodigrass.

I.

It was evening. In the old mission house the frugal supper was over, and the missionary, his wife, the two lady-teachers, the eleven native female boarders and the native probationer, all knelt down to prayers. The eleven boarders and the probationer had come in at the sound of the bell, the eldest boarder leading, and the probationer bringing up the rear.

A few seconds later, the old black housemaid and cook combined strode heavily in and knelt down just inside the door. Prayers over, Miss Elizabeth Blake, the senior lady teacher, sat down to the harmonium and played the first few bars of a hymn. Then the little congregation stood up and sang. They kept good time, and their singing was fairly in tune, but the voices of some of the native girls were very harsh and shrill, and somewhat spoilt the general effect. The probationer, Samuel Gozani, led the singing from his place close to the instrumentalist. The choir stood facing the right-hand end of the harmonium, and the leader stood just on Miss Blake's left hand, and to see the choir he had to look over her head. The hymn happened to be Luther's "Ein feste Burg ist unser Gott"; it was sung in English, but the Reverend Gottlieb Schultz, the missionary, forgetting the English words, drifted into the original German at the second verse, rather to the detriment of the performance. Miss Blake sang out her clear, simple soprano tones, very rich in the low notes. She was a handsome girl, rather stout, with blue eyes and dull yellow hair. Her face was somewhat pale from overwork and want of fresh air. Altogether, she had a strongly Teutonic look, and was, in fact, almost an exact counterpart of what her German mother had been at her age. Of her Irish father she showed absolutely no trace in either appearance or character.

Whilst the hymn was being sung, the probationer's earnest eyes rested as often on the yellow-haired girl at the harmonium as on his particular charge, the dusky choir. The eleven girls stood in a crescent, some modest and demure enough, but others looking bold, their wanton, roving eyes and generously developed figures being much in evidence. The youngest girl might have been twelve years of age, and the eldest twenty. The latter, a girl named Martha Kawa, was of a much lighter colour than any of her schoolmates, but her physiognomy was of the usual Kafir type. Her father was an Englishman, and her mother a Gaika Kafir; she had passed her childhood in a native hut, and when, five years previously, she was sent to the mission, she was in a condition of absolute savagery. In the mission school her Aryan blood told; she kept easily ahead of the other girls, and took all the best prizes.

The hymn over, the girls curtsied "good-night" to the missionary and his wife, and went to the dormitory escorted by the junior teacher. This room was the very picture of neatness. The whitewashed walls were decorated with Biblical pictures and illuminated texts, and the beds, with blue counterpanes and snow-white linen, were without crease or wrinkle. On each bed, near the foot, the occupier's shawl was folded, and the manner of folding varied considerably. Small prizes were given for the best folding designs, and considerable individuality was shown in the competition. Several of the designs were marvels of ingenuity, and indicated a true artistic faculty.

In a few moments, eleven dusky heads were reposing on eleven snowy pillows.

II.

The Reverend Gottlieb Schultz was far more intellectual and cultivated than the average of his class. Sent to labour in the Lord's

Vineyard in reclaiming the heathen of South Africa, immediately after his ordination as a minister of the German Evangelical Church, at the age of twenty-four, he had spent thirty-five years at his task. His wife Amalia, selected for him by the Missionary Society, was sent out under invoice five years after his arrival. She had thus been his helpmeet, and a faithful one, for thirty years. Although childless, she was of a placid and contented disposition; so much so that her smile became rather wearisome from its very continuousness.

The good old missionary had outlived many illusions, and of the few still remaining, the larger proportion related to the Fatherland he had left so long ago and which he never more would see. His passionate loyalty to the Hohenzollerns was, long after the events now recorded had happened, the cause of his removing a resplendent portrait of Bismarck from a prominent place in the dining-room; and hiding it ignominiously behind a book-shelf, where it remained until 1893, when the reconciliation between Emperor William and the ex-chancellor took place. Then the portrait was again brought forth, and hung next to that of Count Caprivi which had supplanted it.

On his top bookshelf, triumphant over a dreary jungle of theological literature, might have been found the works of Goethe, Schiller, Lessing and Freiligrath, and in a secret receptacle behind his little drug cabinet reposed a complete edition of Heine. He was very well read in English theological literature. He thought Luther the greatest of all theologians, but his favourite reading was Tauler. He had an emotional understanding of, and sympathy with, the "Friends of God."

And what illusions had he not outlived! Had he not seen the natives, for whose benefit his blameless and strenuous life had been ungrudgingly spent, sinking lower and lower, exchanging the virtues of barbarism for the vices of civilisation? Had he not seen the chosen lambs of his flock sink back into the savagery that surrounded them, lured by those tribal rites which bear a fundamental resemblance to the ritual of the worship of the Cyprian Venus? Had he not seen the land covered with plague-spots in the shape of canteens from which poisonous liquor was set flowing far and wide, ruining the natives, body and soul? All this and more he had seen; all this and more he had prayed and struggled against through the weary years. He still prayed, but he had almost ceased from struggling.

One illusion he still retained. This was the firm belief that the average barbarian was fully the equal of the average civilised man — an illusion so common amongst the missionary fraternity early in this century, that this equality was almost, if not quite, a fundamental axiom in all missionary reasoning. In Mr. Schultz's case, this illusion had paled from time to time in the face of striking experiences, but it was too deeply ingrained in his character ever to disappear. Experience after experience faded out of his memory, but the fundamental axiom remained. These experiences he, so to say, preached away, for whenever he found the fundamental axiom waxing dim, he polished it up with a liberal administration of theological logic, abstruse reasoning, and illustrations from standard authorities.

Samuel Gozani, the probationer, was in several respects a remarkable character. Son of a native headman of the Gealeka tribe, which considers itself as forming, as it were, the Kafir aristocracy; he had, fourteen years previously, been placed at the mission school. For six years he was as backward in acquirement as he was unsatisfactory and troublesome in conduct. But a change came. A native revivalist visited the mission, and, behold — a shaking! Amongst the dry bones that moved, none showed so much energy as Samuel. His whole life changed, and he at once declared his intention of entering the ministry. He took to theological study with the greatest avidity, and for several years was looked upon as the coming man of the mission. Suddenly he again changed; his moral conduct remained free from reproach, but his faculty for serious study appeared to have left him. He brooded deeply, taught the junior pupils in an irregular and, on the whole, very perfunctory manner, and seemed to be consumed by a deep and abiding sadness. It was afterwards noticed that this change dated from about a year after Miss Blake had taken up her residence at the mission.

Samuel possessed A rich, full baritone voice, and he seemed to regain his old vigour and enthusiasm only on those occasions when he sang in the choir. There his voice rang out clear above the others as he led; his eye flashed, and his countenance lit up. He was a tall and strongly built man, with a face unlike the usual Kafir type. His lips were thin, his nose narrow and prominent, and his eyes large and somewhat protruding. In point of physiognomy, he somewhat resembled a North American Indian.

III.

It was on a warm night in late Spring that Miss Elizabeth Blake sat under the verandah which ran along the whole front of the mission house. A slight thunderstorm had just passed, and another was following on its trail. Summer lightnings were gleaming through the soft haze, and distant thunders muttered from time to time. Brown, furry beetles dashed themselves violently against the windows of the dining-room, where a lamp still burned, and the pneumoras wailed their melancholy love-songs from the willow trees along the water-furrow. The junior teacher was seeing her charges to bed, for prayers were just over, and Miss Blake was enjoying a few moments' rest in the mild air before taking up her task of preparing the next day's work. The missionary and his wife were away, visiting at the next-neighbouring mission, and were not expected back until the following afternoon.

Hearing the sound of approaching footsteps, Miss Blake looked round, and saw Samuel Gozani approaching. He came slowly up the steps, and stood silently before her, leaning against one of the verandah poles.

"Good evening, Samuel, " she said.

"Good evening, Miss Elizabeth; you do not often take a rest. "

"I seldom have time. "

Samuel remained silent, and the girl regarded him intently. She had long noticed his demeanour, and had often wondered as to what was on his mind.

"Samuel, " she said, sympathetically, "why have you been so strange of late? Is anything the matter with you? "

Samuel cleared his throat as if to speak, shifted his feet, but said nothing.

"Do you not know, " she continued, "that your class is going backward, that you often forget to set the lessons, and that half the time you are teaching you appear as if you do not know what you are doing? Tell me, is there anything on your mind? Have you done anything you are sorry for? "

Samuel again cleared his throat, shifted his feet, and with an evident effort replied:

"I have not committed any sin, but I know my work is done badly. My heart is so heavy that I can hardly bear the weight. "

"What is this heaviness? "

Samuel did not reply, but after a pause asked this question:

"Miss Elizabeth, do you believe that all men, white and black, are equal? "

The girl paused for a moment. In her heart of hearts she knew she did not think so, but the fundamental axiom weighed heavily on her, the well-worn arguments of the missionary arose and threatened her, pointing with skinny fingers at the abyss which lay in the road of the opposite view, so she muffled her answer up carefully in a platitude, and handed it to her hearer, trusting that the muffler would somewhat conceal its nakedness.

"Of course, " she said, "the bad are not equal to the good; but if God holds that otherwise all men are equal, it would be wrong of any one to think differently. "

"But white people never really think that we blacks are equal to them, " said Samuel, speaking in a strained tone, "no matter what they say. "

Miss Blake felt unable to reply, so after a short pause Samuel continued:

"When a black man walks in the ways of the whites, he becomes a stranger to his own kind, and he has really no friends. The white man says 'Come here to us, ' and when the black man comes as near as he can, there is still a gulf that he cannot pass. I am a lonely man, Miss Elizabeth; I have left my own people, and there is no one that I can call a friend. Even you only tolerate me because you think it pleasing to God that you should do so; but you would never be my friend or let me be yours. "

"There you are wrong, Samuel, " replied the girl, moved by a sense of great pity; "I have the warmest friendship and regard for you, and I like you as well as if you were white. "

Samuel then did an unusual thing—he held out his hand to the girl, who took it and pressed it cordially.

"Good night. Miss Elizabeth, " he said. "I will do my duty better, and try to be worthy of your friendship. You have lightened my heart. "

Miss Blake went in to the empty class-room and arranged the morrow's work. She was filled with a vague sense of uneasiness, and she felt that in her conversation with Samuel she had not been quite ingenuous; especially in her closing remark.

Samuel went to his room, and, as was his wont, read several chapters of the Bible before going to bed. On this occasion his choice fell upon the Song of Solomon. This he read right through. He began it again, and read until he reached the words, "I am black but comely. " He went to sleep with these words on his lips, and with a strange dream at his heart.

IV.

The mission was perplexed by another change in Samuel. He bought a new suit of clothes; he parted his hair on the left side, teasing it up into two high, unequal ridges; he became redolent of cheap scent; he applied himself anew to his studies, with feverish activity, and he pulled his disorderly class together so effectively, that when the school inspector again came to the mission, that official dealt out almost unstinted praise instead of the censure which was usually Samuel's well-deserved portion.

Moreover, Samuel notified his intention of qualifying forthwith for his next step towards the ministry. In the choir, his voice rang out with an almost birdlike rapture that astonished all hearers.

It was then noticed that Martha Kawa began to lose her place at the top of the class. It should be mentioned that all the boarders, as well as the senior day pupils, were taught by Miss Blake, and that Samuel taught the second class. The very small pupils were instructed by the second lady-teacher. Martha grew thin and ill-tempered. On several occasions she was very impertinent to Miss Blake. In church, or when singing after evening prayers, she hardly ever took her eyes from Samuel. This was, of course, remarked by the other girls, but a chaffing allusion to the fact was met by such a burst of fury, that the experiment was not repeated.

Samuel hardly ever spoke to Miss Blake; in fact he appeared to avoid her. His usual taciturnity was unchanged, but it did not convey the idea of moroseness. His general demeanour was as that of one in a dream, but in Miss Blake's presence he became alert, with almost an expectant look; and he gave, generally, the idea of being under the influence of strong, but suppressed excitement.

Miss Blake was very fond of flowers, and on the hills around the mission, watsonias, purple orchids, and other flowers grew; whilst on the edges of the kloofs, sweet-scented clematis trailed. Samuel got into the habit of gathering flowers—generally on Saturday afternoons, when he was free from duty. After one of his rambles, a bouquet would generally be sent to each of the teachers and to Mrs. Schultz, but it was noticed that the choicest selection always reached the senior teacher.

The Reverend Robley Wilson, a young Wesleyan minister who had been ordained three years previously, became a more or less constant visitor at the mission. He was in charge of a station about thirty miles distant. A tall, spare man, with dark eyes and hair, he had the reputation of being extremely shrewd. Belonging to the more modern school, the fundamental axiom did not weigh heavily upon him; in fact it was hardly a burthen at all, but rather a cloak that could be donned or doffed as occasion demanded.

Mr. Wilson's attentions to the senior teacher became somewhat marked. Strange to say, this fact appeared to be quite unnoticed by Samuel, who still pursued his course of feverish study, and became more and more abstracted in his manner. The unhappy man was consumed by a passionate love. It was for Miss Blake that he was striving to qualify as a minister; it was of her that he thought all day and dreamt all night. Into his wild and elemental nature, in which hereditary savagery was simply covered by a thin veneer of civilisation, this strong love for a woman of an alien race had struck its roots deep down, and absorbed all into itself. But instead of the savage element being transmuted into gentleness, his love absorbed into itself the savage, and thus became savage in its character. This resultant was a highly explosive psychic compound. He never spoke to another being of what his mind was full of, and the repression which he had to exercise at all natural vents caused tidal waves of passion to roll back on his soul, fraught with destruction to himself and to others.

Martha Kawa was as passionately attached to Samuel, as he was to Miss Blake. In Martha, the Aryan element manifested itself mainly in force of character, and ability; for in her tastes and desires, as in her physiognomy, she followed her mother's race. Whilst Samuel was secretive by nature, she was rendered so by force of circumstances; she had hardly any opportunities of communicating with the man she loved, and on the rare occasions when she diffidently attempted to gain his confidence and friendship, she was met by a cold and impenetrable indifference, She was not on terms of intimacy with any of the other pupils, the fact of her being partly of another race preventing anything of the kind.

It will be seen that the moral and social atmosphere of the mission was heavily charged with tragic potentialities.

V.

In course of time, Miss Blake went away to spend her Christmas holidays at a distant town, her native place. The Reverend Robley Wilson took a holiday shortly afterwards, and followed her. He asked her to be a helpmeet unto him, and she agreed. Whatever love existed between them was mainly on his side. She came back to the mission engaged, but by agreement the fact was to be kept secret for a time, even from the Missionary and his wife.

During the holidays, Samuel had continued his course of feverish study. His face had become thin and drawn, and his eyes looked unnaturally bright and prominent. Martha was more ill-tempered and sulky than ever, and repeated disobedience had led to talk of her expulsion. During the holidays she had volunteered to stay at the mission rather than go back to her mother's kraal. She was allowed to stay on condition that she did the house-work, helping the old domestic, who was far from well. She thus had many opportunities of cultivating Samuel's acquaintance, and it was not long before her suspicions as to his passion for Miss Blake were fully confirmed. Samuel allowed her to talk to him, but he said very little in reply.

About a week after Miss Blake's return, Mr. Wilson managed to get an invitation to preach at the mission on the following Sunday. He arrived on Friday, and then, for the first time, Samuel began to suspect the true state of affairs. On Saturday evening Miss Blake and her lover were sitting together in a little summer-house in the garden, Samuel had watched them enter and then, stealthily as a cat, had crept up to the trellis, and taken a position where he could hear every word spoken. What he heard left no room for any doubt as to the true state of affairs. At first he felt as if stunned by the shock, the very force of the blow precluding suffering for the time being. The mention of his own name brought him to himself, and every word of the conversation that followed burned itself into his brain.

"What a strange character that Samuel Gozani is, " said Mr. Wilson; "I have sometimes thought him slightly mad. "

"So have I, " replied the girl, and she then gave a rapid sketch of Samuel's career at the mission.

"Has it never struck you that he may have presumed to fall in love with you? "

"I do not like to speak about such a thing, but it has; and for some time back I have hardly been able to bear his presence. I shudder whenever he comes near me. "

"I think it is such a mistake to let these fellows think they can be on an equality with us, " said Mr. Wilson, after a pause; "it always leads to unpleasantness. The idea of his presuming even to think of you in that way. "

"I often recall his asking me such a strange question one night last year. He asked if I thought all men, black and white, were equal, It was not so much the question, as his manner of putting it, that struck me as being strange. "

"And what did you say in reply? "

"Oh, I said that before God all men were equal. He then asked whether I thought one who was white could ever look on a black man as really his equal. I did not like to say what I truly thought, and felt, so I made an evasive answer. "

"I know old Schultz and his school teach a lot of nonsense on that point, " said Mr. Wilson, scornfully, "although none of them truly believe what they say. The equality idea is quite an exploded one, and the black savage, superficially civilised, is no more the equal of the European, than a Basuto pony is equal to a thoroughbred horse. But I hope you will keep that fellow in his place! "

"Yes, of course I will. But I pity him nevertheless. "

"Do you? I cannot say that I do. But after all, he is not so much to blame as is the system which filled his head with nonsense. These old missionaries have done a lot of harm in giving the natives false notions as to equality, and making them generally conceited. "

Samuel had heard enough. He crept away as noiselessly as he came.

Next day the Rev. Robley Wilson preached one of his very best sermons. His preaching was ex tempore, and full of vigour. He discoursed of righteousness, of temperance, and of judgment to come on the unrighteous and the intemperate. He waxed more and more didactic. He called upon his hearers to thank the Lord that such men as he, the Reverend Robley Wilson, had thought fit to devote their lives to the service of the children of Ham, instead of shining in metropolitan pulpits and pouring vials of saving grace over the heads of the elect of the children of Shem. He dwelt on the inconveniences of mission life in South Africa, and drew a moving picture of the contrast between such, and existence in a civilised, European city—comforted by the appliances of Science and cheered by the achievements of Art. He again called upon the children of Ham to thank their common Maker for the blessings bestowed on them by the children of Shem, and he wound up with a prayer so audaciously comprehensive, that had all thereby asked for been granted, the members of the congregation, and all their friends and relations—to say nothing of the whole human race which was included in a general clause—would have had nothing more to hope for, and must have succumbed to sheer repletion. It was a rousing sermon, but it contained not a single reference to the fundamental axiom.

Whilst the blessings conferred upon the natives by the Europeans were being enumerated, Miss Blake (quite involuntarily) thought of the canteens in the village close at hand, coming from which, drunken men and women often staggered past; the mission, and during the fascinating description of life in a European city, she could not help recalling certain accounts she had recently read of the experiences of venturesome persons who explored regions called slums, said to exist to a considerable extent in most large British cities. But it was a rousing sermon; and well delivered.

Samuel led the choir, and his voice had, if possible, a more exultant and triumphant ring than usual.

At evening service, the old missionary preached—or rather read his sermon. His was a much humbler effort than that of his locum tenens of the forenoon, but it left a more salutary and peaceful impression. None of the ideas were original, the illustrations were commonplace, and what passed for argument was rather threadbare. The fundamental axiom was there, but was not aggressively flaunted: it was rather implied than expressed. But in spite of all this, the hearers, or most of them, were the better of the discourse, for the simple loving kindness and faith of the old man permeated the congregation as a gentle and soothing influence.

It was noticed that Samuel withdrew quietly from the church just at the close of the last hymn, and before the final prayer and blessing. When the junior teacher assembled the girls a few minutes later, in the dormitory, Martha Kawa was missing.

The Reverend Robley Wilson and Miss Blake lingered in the church for a few minutes after the congregation had left, and strolled together across the grass plot to the Mission House. At the door, Mr. Wilson excused himself, and walked down through the shrubbery towards the visitors's house—a little one-roomed building, set apart for guests. He meant just to leave his Bible and hymnbook on the table, brush his hair, and then rejoin Miss Blake and the others in the dining-room, where supper awaited them. He softly whistled the tune of a hymn as he went along the path, thinking how very inconvenient it was that he had to return home on the following day. It had been agreed that the engagement was to be announced that evening to the kind old missionary and his wife. He also thought of the inevitable opposition to a short engagement, as he knew how difficult it would be to find a suitable successor to Miss Blake. He had just begun to compare the sermon he had just been listening to with his own of the morning—much to the disadvantage of the former, through which he could perceive the fundamental axiom protruding like a cloven foot, when he suddenly ceased thinking for ever, for a blow from the heavy knob of a strong stick crushed his skull in on his brain like an egg-shell, and he sank, a limp mass, to the ground.

Then Samuel Gozani, for it was his arm that had struck the blow, sprang from the footpath into the thickest part of the shrubbery, and there came into violent physical contact with Martha Kawa, who had been a witness of his murderous deed.

They waited in the dining-room, expecting the arrival of the guest, and wondering at his long absence. Suddenly a loud shriek was heard coming from the direction of the shrubbery, and the missionary left the dining-room and walked quickly down the passage to the front door, which Stood wide open. There he met Martha Kawa, whose demeanour showed signs of the most frantic terror. Her face was of a dull, ash colour; her mouth hung open and her eyes were dilated. She gasped for breath, pointed towards the visitors' house, and then sank senseless to the ground. The missionary returned to the dining-room, seized a candle, and walked quickly down the shrubbery path, the flame of the candle hardly flickering in the breathless night air. There was the body, a huddled mass, lying on its face, with the arms stretched out at right angles, and the palms of the bands turned upwards. A trickle of blood ran down the slope for a few inches, and then formed a pool. The poor old man stood for a few moments transfixed with horror, and then staggered back to the house.

Shortly afterwards the shrubbery was full of blanched faces, rendered doubly ghastly by the faint glimmer of the lanterns and candles. Samuel was there, taciturn as usual, and the most self-possessed person present. He came direct from his room when the alarm was given. Miss Blake was led by Mrs. Schultz into the house. Then hands, tremulous with terror and pity, lifted tenderly what had so recently been a human being brimming with youthful, healthy life, and exalted with anticipation of the crown of happy love, and laid it on the little white bed. Later, when the officials came to view the body, they opened the door softly and shrinkingly, and the drip, drip, drip on the clay floor sounded on their tense brains like strokes from the hammer of doom.

When Martha Kawa had sufficiently recovered to be capable of answering questions, she told a strange story. She had heard, so she said, a voice raised as though in anger, but had been unable to distinguish the words, and just afterwards a dull thud. She then walked quickly towards where these sounds had come from, and was just able to distinguish two men running away. This was all that could be elicited from her.

Suspicion at once fell upon Samuel. In his room was found a large knobbed stick, such as might have caused the wound, with the knob still damp, apparently from recent washing. Foot-marks corresponding with his were found in suspicious localities in the shrubbery. He was arrested and tried for the crime, but was acquitted on the evidence of Martha Kawa. When, shortly after the trial, Samuel and Martha disappeared simultaneously, every one felt that Samuel was surely guilty, and that his acquittal, which was irrevocable, had involved a terrible miscarriage of justice.

Miss Blake left the mission and returned to her family. Mr. Schultz shortly afterwards retired from active work, and went to live in one of the larger colonial towns. He drew a small pension which, with the interest upon the scanty savings of his charitable life, was sufficient for his moderate needs. He still holds by the fundamental axiom.

VI.

About three years after the tragedy just related, a native man and woman lived together in a lonely hut close to the mouth of the Bashee river, They were clad in the savage garb common to the uncivilised natives. The woman was of a much lighter complexion than the man, and she carried, slung on her back, an emaciated child with a badly deformed spine. On her face and body were many scars, most of them healed up, but some still raw, and evidently of recent infliction. Samuel Gozani and Martha Kawa had wandered far since leaving the mission. They had gone together to the kraal of the headman, Samuel's father, in Gealekaland, but Samuel's violent temper had led to his being driven away. His father gave him a few goats, and his other relations told him to depart and return no more. So he and Martha built a hut far from other men, and cultivated a small field of maize, millet, and pumpkins. Samuel's temper grew worse under the stress of his solitary life, and Martha suffered much from his ill-treatment. Shortly after an act of particularly brutal violence on his part she was confined, and the poor little baby, a boy, was found to be hopelessly deformed. According to native custom, such a child would have been destroyed, but when Samuel suggested this, the mother blazed out into such wrath that he did not refer to the subject again. It soon became apparent that Samuel—sometimes, at least—was insane. He seemed hardly ever to sleep, and he remained days without speaking, One day, on entering the hut, he savagely kicked the child, which was lying on a mat just inside the door, to one side. The poor little thing set up a thin, piteous squeal, which, when the mother heard it, roused her to a pitch of tiger-like fury. She rushed at Samuel and flung him backwards out of the door. Incensed to madness, he sprang at her, dashed her down on the floor, and held her with his hands at her throat, and his knees pressing violently on her stomach. He held her thus for some seconds, then sprang up, rushed out of the hut, and disappeared into the bush.

The wretched woman lay senseless for some time, and when she regained consciousness she felt that she had sustained some serious internal injury. It was early in the forenoon when the deed was done, and in the afternoon her body began to swell, and she suffered violent pain. She had, as a matter of fact, sustained a severe internal rupture. She managed to crawl over to where the child lay, still wailing, and she gave it the breast to still it. Then she began to suffer from violent thirst, but there was neither water nor milk in the hut. Owing to Samuel's bad reputation no one ever came to his dwelling, and thus Martha had no chance of succour before his return, which she now longed for. The sun went down, and she lay in agony, watching the dying daylight. She lay through the long, slow hours of the night, unable to move, and with the poor little child tugging at her in vain, and fitfully wailing from hunger and cold, for the fire had long since gone out. When morning broke she became delirious; later on she became unconscious, and remained so all day. When Samuel returned at sundown, driving home the little flock of goats, she appeared to be at the last gasp. He was, to do him justice, much shocked at what he saw. Samuel at once ran down to the river and fetched some water, a little of which, poured down Martha's parched throat, restored her to consciousness. He lit a fire and sat down near her, giving her a sip of water now and then. He even wrapped the child up in a tanned calf skin, and then went out and caught a she-goat, which he flung to the ground, and tied by its extended legs to two poles of the hut, which were about six feet apart. He then placed the chilled and starving child where it could suck one of the teats. The goat struggled and withheld its milk, but Samuel held it down and kneaded the udder until the draught came, and the child drank long and deeply.

When the mother saw this, she smiled faintly, and just afterwards she fell quietly asleep. The child also slept, so Samuel released the goat and returned to his seat.

The fire flickered up and showed by fits and starts the inside of the hut. There lay the dying woman, her deathlike face drawn and haggard from her long agony, breathing very shortly, the beginning of the death rattle being audible. There lay the child, half covered by the skin, its lips parted in the ghastly semblance of a smile which was due to the indigestion caused by a heavy meal of unusual food, and there sat Samuel with wide open eyes, looking down into the fire without seeing it.

Outside the stars glittered down through the cool June air upon the lovely valley, rich in forest and flanked by gently-swelling, grassy hills. The tinkling murmur of the river which, after rainless months, had shrunk to the dimensions of a streamlet, except in the long, deep reaches, stole up from where it ran, crystal clear, over a low, rocky bar.

Suddenly Martha opened her eyes and spoke in a thin, far-away voice—

"Samuel."

He started, and, moving to where she lay, bent over her.

"Samuel," she said, "I am dying—now! now!" (She spoke English, a thing neither of them had done since they had left the mission.) "Perhaps it is true—what they used to teach us—perhaps Jesus did die for us. —Samuel—I love you—and you have killed me—but if I find— Jesus—I will ask—him—to let you come!"

She gasped, and stopped speaking, and just then the child woke up and wailed. This seemed to electrify her.

"Oh, God! the child!" she screamed. "Give him to me!"

Samuel arose, gently lifted the wailing baby, and laid it on her left side, between her arm and her body, with its head on her shoulder.

"Samuel—Samuel, " she gasped, "I lied—to save—you. It is—your—child. We have been—bad—but Jesus—will forgive. He will—forgive—us both—if you—take care——"

Here her breath failed, and she struggled painfully to speak, her eyes becoming dim and bright by turns. She tried to lift her right hand, but could not, so she turned it on its back and beckoned with the forefinger. Samuel gently laid his hand in hers, and she slowly grasped his fingers. She lay still like this for a time; hardly breathing, and with that strange, fitful gleam coming back at longer intervals to her dimming eyes. Suddenly her eyes flashed almost fiercely, and, with what must have been a terrible effort, she drew his hand across her body until it rested on the child's head. She held it there until she died.

In the morning Samuel again caught the she-goat, carried it into the hut, laid it down, and bound its legs as he had previously done. But the child would not drink. About midday the poor little thing began to scream violently, and at sundown it died in strong convulsions, Samuel holding it tenderly in his arms.

At midnight Samuel buried the two bodies together in a shallow grave, over which he piled a quantity of heavy stones to keep off the jackals. He then went to the little kraal where the goats were kept, and pulled away the bush which served as a gate, thus leaving the entrance open. He then divested himself of every article of clothing and ornament, and placed them in the hut. The fire had gone out, but, after raking about deep down in the pile of ashes, he found a few embers still alight. These he placed carefully on a bent wisp of dry grass which he pulled out of the roof, and which blazed up in a few seconds. He then set fire to the hut in several places, and went outside. In a few minutes the hut, being built of wattles and grass, all now as dry as tinder, blazed up. Samuel stood and watched the fire until the last flame flickered out. He then turned his back on the heap of glowing embers, and walked away in the direction of the river.

There is a deep pool in the river a few hundred yards from the spot where Samuel's hut used to stand, and at one side of it the bank rises precipitously for about twenty feet. Upon this bank stood Samuel Gozani, naked as he was born, and he lifted up his voice and spake:

"The white men told me about a God that died for all men, and that rewards the good and punishes the wicked, but the white man lied about other things, so I cannot believe him. My father told me about Tikoloshe, who lives in the water, and pulls people down by the feet into the darkness. I never knew my father to lie; I want to reach the darkness, so I will go to Tikoloshe. "

He sprang into the pool, and Tikoloshe pulled him down by the feet into the darkness.

KELLSON'S NEMESIS.

"Take Sin's empty goblet, fling it
Hurtling from some sheer cliff's height,
Winds will bear it up and wing it
Back to thee in devious flight.
Smash it against the rocks—before thee
Laming fragments strew thy path.
Swamp it deep—the waves restore thee
What thou gav'st them, brimmed with wrath."

SHAGBAG'S Soliloquy on the Boomerang.

Night had fallen, although the red glow had not yet quite faded out of the west, when John Jukes Kellson, the newly appointed Civil Commissioner and Resident Magistrate of Marsonton, drove down the hill into the village in which he would henceforth reside and exercise his official functions. The cart drawn by four horses, which conveyed him, had been hired at a town over ninety miles away, and Kellson had driven that distance in two broiling hot days. As the cart went slowly down the hill, the moon was rising over the eastern mountains, and a breathless stillness reigned, broken only by the rumble of the vehicle. How familiar it all was; he knew every curve of the road and every ant-heap; every bush looming in the twilight seemed like an old acquaintance. Nineteen years had passed since Kellson had last seen the village. A clerk in the local public offices, he had left it on promotion, and now he was returning as chief Government functionary. How strange it seemed.

The cart reached the hotel and stopped before the front door. It was Sunday night. Having a constitutional distaste for public functions of all kinds, outside the established official routine, Kellson had purposely left the inhabitants of the village and district in the dark as to the date of his intended arrival, so as to avoid the agonies of a public reception, involving an address and a reply, both couched in the irritating platitudinous phraseology deemed indispensable on such occasions.

He entered the hotel at which he had formerly boarded and lodged for several years as a bachelor. The faces he saw were all strange, but the building was just the same. It was evident that neither the doors, the windows, nor the verandah had been renewed since he had seen the place last. The same atmosphere of mustiness permeated the premises; the ill-laid flags forming the floor of the stoep still with lifted edges lay in wait for unaccustomed feet. He knew those flags, and the old habit of stepping high when he walked on them returned. He even remembered, as he walked along, the places where it was safe to tread and those to be avoided.

The servant showed him to his room, the same he had occupied twenty years ago. Twenty years; good God! what a long time. He was then twenty-six years old—and now. How many things had happened in those years. The servant lit the candle, and Kellson looked round the room. Yes; just as he had expected; there was the same furniture. The wall-paper was different, that was all. He passed his hand over the foot of the iron bedstead and drew out one of the slides of the old, rickety chest of drawers. How many people had slept in that bed since that morning when he had here packed his portmanteau before carrying it out to the post-cart.

He went to supper, and recognised familiar objects at every turn. These recognitions hurt him so much that he could hardly keep from crying out. He feared to lift his eyes lest he should see some old acquaintance in the shape of a fly-blown picture grinning at him. The proprietor of the hotel and his family were all absent at church, and for this small mercy Kellson was devoutly thankful. Supper over, he strolled out into the silent village street. He could not, however, endure the sensations which he experienced, so he hurried back to his room. The transfiguring moonlight had conjured up the ghost of his youth, and it mocked and gibed at him cruelly.

Kellson was a bad sleeper, but he went to bed early so as to rest his weary limbs. He lit his pipe, and then tried to read, but the mists of nineteen years gathered between his eyes and the page, so he blew out the candle and lay still with his eyes wide open and no thought of sleep. The whole weight of the past seemed to press on and crush him, whilst the stress of the present prevented his dropping the load and resting. Moreover, numbers of those wretched cur dogs that swarm in most South African villages were now barking in all directions, the full moon and the warm night drawing out more than the usual contingent.

Kellson's official residence was on a hill just beyond the other end of the village, and he determined, without waiting for the arrival of the waggons with his effects, to buy next day enough furniture for one small bedroom which he would occupy, still taking his meals at the hotel. He would thus be away from the horrible dogs. He meant to board at the hotel until the arrival of his wife. His wife t why must he think of her with such bitterness? Why must he look forward to her return from her trip to Europe with uneasiness and dissatisfaction? It was the old story—incompatibility of temper, or rather of temperament. He had married at the age of thirty-eight, nine years ago. His wife was now twenty-eight. She was one of those women who can be got at only through their feelings—never through their reason. In her a passionate longing for motherhood had absorbed every other wish. She had money of her own and had gone to spend a year in Europe. When she left, Kellson experienced a deep sense of relief; a whole year's freedom seemed endless at the beginning, but now two-thirds of the time had gone by swiftly, and in about four months she would be back. How he dreaded her return and the recommencement of the old discordant life. Kellson was, no doubt, in some respects a difficult man to live with, but he nevertheless would have made a reasonable, sympathetic woman moderately happy. His habit was to act reasonably according to his lights in all his daily relations, both official and domestic. His wife was an extremely emotional person, who could be persuaded to do a thing, or leave it undone, as the case might be, by arguments based upon conventionalism or generosity, but never by those drawn from justice or reasonableness. Kellson had at first set himself the task of showing her the saving graces of reasonableness, but he soon gave the attempt up in disgust. But things would have come all right between them had there only been a child.

Kellson had not been a successful man. At the beginning, his career promised well. Fifteen years previously he had been ahead of most men of his own term of service, but now others—some of them considerably his juniors—had forged past him. He had noticed all his life that he seldom carried any important enterprise to a successful conclusion. Up to a certain point, he usually achieved rapid success, but then difficulties unseen before arose one after the other, and failure, or else only success very much qualified, resulted. He had often endeavoured to find out the reason of this, but had not been able to do so. He came to the conclusion that there was some weak strand in the fibre of his character, but where this lay, or how to strengthen it, he was unable to discover or devise.

His transfer to Marsonton, although it involved no curtailment of salary, was really a reduction in point of status. At his last station he had taken a stand upon a matter in which the prejudices of a large and influential class had been against him. The Government considered he had been injudicious, and transferred him. He did not much mind; all that troubled him, was the nuisance involved in packing up and moving his books and furniture. His conscience was quite clear; he had done what he thought to be his duty. Yet he was honest enough to admit that however right the abstract principle was, its application in the particular circumstances involved may have been injudicious. His ideal of official responsibility was a very high one, and during the whole twenty-seven years of his service he had never done a shady thing; neither had he ever allowed fear of the consequences to deter him from pursuing what he considered to be the right course.

All things come to an end, and so did that Sunday night which Kellson spent at the hotel. In the early morning he took a brighter view of things. After breakfast he went up to the Public Offices, and, to the astonishment of the clerks, introduced himself as their new chief. He had not mentioned who he was at the hotel, and consequently no one knew of his arrival. It being Monday, there was a heavy roll of cases for trial, and when the one attorney and the two agents saw Kellson take the bench, they were much chagrined at having been done out of the pleasure of presenting the usual florid address.

Of the criminal cases to be heard, only one was of any importance, namely that of a young coloured man charged with burglary. His name was John Erlank. He had evidently more of European than of any other blood in his veins; his hair was straight and black, and his complexion light yellow. But the most striking thing about him was the beauty of his eyes. They were black, large and deep. Although clearly showing signs of vice and dissipation, there was something prepossessing in his appearance; a kind of natural refinement was visible through his evident degradation and in spite of his obviously cringing manner. Kellson could not imagine whose face it was that the prisoner's suggested. Although little more than a lad, Erlank had a bad record. From early youth upwards he had been a criminal, and several convictions for different crimes were now formally proved against him. He had in this particular instance been committed to take his trial before the circuit judge by the previous magistrate, before whom he had fully admitted his guilt, but the Attorney General had now remitted the case hack to the magistrate's court for disposal under the "Extended Jurisdiction Act. " Guilt being fully admitted by the prisoner, all Kellson had to do as magistrate was to read over the depositions and pass sentence. He considered the case to be one in which severity was due, so after telling the man he was one on whom exhortation or advice would be thrown away, he passed the highest sentence allowed by law, that is two years' imprisonment with hard labour and a flogging of thirty-six lashes. It was characteristic of Kellson that the prisoner's prepossessing appearance had the involuntary effect of making the sentence more severe, or rather, perhaps, of making the magistrate more stern in his estimate of the criminality.

At about four o'clock, Kellson had disposed of all the cases, and was thus free for the rest of the afternoon, so he left the office and walked up towards his official residence. He had asked the Chief Constable to see to the fitting up of his room, and he now went to look over the premises. For a long time he was unable to dismiss the face of the prisoner Erlank from his memory, it seemed to be almost as familiar to him as the houses of the street along which he was walking.

The village had hardly changed since he had last seen it. It is one of those places that do not grow because they happen not to be on any one of the great highways to the North. One or two old fogeys came up and greeted Kellson in the street—men he had known well in the old days, now so changed as to be almost unrecognisable. He passed the little room which had been used in the old days as a public library and reading-room. It was now shut up, and almost in ruins. He thought of how he used to run over from the office and flirt with the librarian, a very pretty girl, long since married. He passed another house and caught his breath short. It was that in which she had lived—the girl he had loved in his youth, and who had loved him. He had left her in a state of uncertainty as to his intentions, and after keeping up a warm correspondence for some time, they had gradually become estranged, the estrangement commencing on his side. Why had he acted like this, he asked himself bitterly. He had dreaded something or another, he could not quite define what it was. He remembered how she, who had been as Steel to others, was like wax in his hands. He remembered——Ah, God what a lot he remembered.

He arrived at the residency after walking up the hill. The exercise made him puff. In the old days he used to run up steeper gradients, now it sometimes distressed him to walk on level ground.

The gate and the fence were new, but the verandah, the door and the windows, as in the case of the hotel, were the same he had known in the old days. He opened the door and walked in, his footsteps sounding hollow in the empty house.

Kellson stood in the passage. He had left the front door wide open so as to admit the light. The air of the empty house seemed dense with the essence of the past. He went into every room, pausing for a few seconds in each, and then entering the next on tip-toe. He stood in the dining-room, before the fireplace. He had sat where he now stood on so many evenings of winter days whose suns had set with his youth. The barren hearth was full of ghostly flames which struck a chill into his heart. There was the room opening to the left, which Mabel and Vi, the little twin daughters of his former chief, used to occupy. He seemed to hear the laughter of the children echoing from some far-off paradise of the past, before the portal of which a stern-browed Fate stood to prevent his entering. The shutters of the dining-room window had been thrown open. A memory-ghost prompted him to unfold one of them. On its inner surface, painted over, he found the heads of the tacks with which he had nailed the programme of the farewell dance given in honour of his promotion by his chief. Where were the dancers? Gone like the music to which their feet had kept time.

His bed had been placed in the room formerly occupied by the children. This pleased him; the ghosts of Mabel and Vi were more bearable than the other ghosts. He looked in to see that all he required had been provided, and then he walked over the premises outside, old recollections smiting him like whips at every turn. He went into the stable and touched the ring to which "Bob, " an old pony, the joint property of the two little girls, used to be tied. The tennis-ground was over-grown with grass—his predecessor's family evidently had not cared about tennis. He recognised most of the trees in the garden. The old vine at the side of the house was green and full of unripe grapes. It was the only thing that had a cheerful look.

Kellson returned to the hotel, and found that several of the inhabitants of the village had called and left cards. After supper, he walked up again to the residency, and found the Chief Constable there, he having come to see whether the arrangements made were satisfactory. Kellson was much relieved to find he had company. He had dreaded entering the house alone in the dark. There was an old rustic seat under the verandah, and on this Kellson and the Chief Constable sat and talked for half an hour. Then the latter said "Good night" and left.

Kellson remained sitting on the rustic seat, feeling in a better frame of mind. The Moon rose over the big mountain in front of the house and distant about five miles. The soft moonlight made the landscape wonderfully beautiful. The whole mountain was draped in snow-while, clinging mist, except the very summit, over which the Moon was hanging. The peacefulness of the hour stole into his heart, and his brain calmed down. The mountain suggested to him the past, and the pure, white mist shrouding it seemed like vapour risen from the merciful waters of Lethe. The Moon suggested hope, vague and undefined, lint still hope. With the swing as of a pendulum his consciousness swept back from the dark night of despondency and bathed its wings in light. Then his soothed spirit felt the need of sleep, so he entered the house and began to prepare for bed.

The waggon-road from the village scarped around the slope at the back of the house, and he heard the clatter of a waggon passing along it. The noise irritated him sorely—he could not tell why. Soon it ceased, and he wondered why the waggon should have stopped where it did. A few minutes afterwards he heard the sound of approaching footsteps, so he paused in his undressing, wondering irritably who was coming to disturb him. Then he heard a light tap at the front door.

Taking a candle, he went to the door and opened it. He saw before him a woman. She was coloured, but of mixed race, the European element evidently preponderating. She was elderly—certainly over forty years of age—very thin; and she stooped somewhat. Her face was drawn and haggard, but her eyes were still beautiful—black, large, and deep. She was decently but poorly dressed.

"Good evening, sir, " she said, speaking Dutch.

"Good evening, " replied Kellson. "What do you want? "

"I beg your pardon. Sir, coming at this time to trouble you. I only came because I am in great grief. But do you not know me? "

"No, " said Kellson, after scanning her features carefully; "I do not remember you. What is your name? "

"I am Rachel, sir."

"Rachel," he said, sharply; "not Rachel Arends?"

"Yes, Sir, I was Rachel Arends, but I married Martin Erlank, the blacksmith of Ratel Hoek, just after you left, long ago."

Kellson turned sick at heart. Here was a reminder of a thing he had fain forgotten, come to drive away the peace he had just acquired. Here was the ghost of a sin of long ago, which had put on flesh and blood and come back to haunt him. It was horrible. He looked at the woman— she returned his gaze timidly for a moment, and then humbly drooped her head. Her manner and attitude suggested woe and utter humility. Then a wave of kindness and pity swept through him. Here was a fellow-creature with whom he had tasted the sweets of sin, long ago. Her youth, and all of her that he remembered, had been left behind by the hurrying years. Only one thing was clear, she was in trouble and she wanted his help. He would succour her if he could.

"Come in," he said to her kindly; and she followed him into the empty dining-room. He closed the shutters, and placed the candle on the window-sill. Then he fetched the only two chairs out of his bedroom. He placed one for her, and sat in the other himself.

"Now, Rachel," he said in a kind voice, "what can I do for you?"

Rachel tried to speak, but sobs choked her. Kellson sat and watched her, trying to imagine the course of the change in her appearance through the nineteen years. Where had her beauty gone to—the clear yellow of her cheeks, through which the red seemed to burn, making them look like ripe nectarines. Where was her graciously curved bosom? Ah! "Where are the snows of yester-year?"

"Oh, Sir," she said at length, "I have come to you about my son whom you punished today."

Kellson now for the first time remembered that the surname she had given him was the same as that of the prisoner whom he had so severely sentenced. He could now decipher the suggestion in the eyes, which had so puzzled him.

"Was that your son?" he asked.

"Yes, Sir. I know he is bad, and it is his conduct that has made an old woman of me. But I thought you might do something for him. I do not mind about the two years' imprisonment—that may do him good—but the thirty-six lashes."

"Oh, Sir, his skin has always been so tender, ever since he was a little baby. It is quite white and soft under his shirt. For the love of God, do not flog him. I did not know he was to be tried to-day, or I would have come before. When I heard you were coming I felt sure he would have had mercy."

"My poor woman," said Kellson, his heart pierced by Rachel's agony, "what can I do? I have no power to alter the sentence. He had been convicted so often before that I felt bound to punish him severely."

"I know. I know he deserves it, but for the love of God, take off the lashes. Oh, Sir, you cannot flog him. Bad as he is, I love him best of all my children, and all the others are good."

"What can I do?" said Kellson, deeply distressed. "The sentence is passed. I have no power to change it."

"Oh, Sir, do you not understand—must I tell you? I thought you would have known."

"What do you mean?"

Rachel again burst into violent weeping, and swayed to and fro in her chair. For some time she could not speak, Kellson sat and looked at her, a vague feeling of uneasiness stirring in him. At length she became calmer, and sat still—her hands pressed to her face. She stood up, looked fixedly at Kellson for a moment, and then fell un her knees before him.

"Save him, save him from the flogging," she said hoarsely, "he is your son."

Kellson sprang to his feet and looked down at the kneeling woman; his eyes stony with horror, and his face white and rigid. He knew in a flash that what she said was true. The face that the prisoner's reminded him of, and that he could not localise, was his own. Several peculiarities in the prisoner's appearance now struck him. It was quite clear—as sure as death and as obvious as his sin. He had sentenced his own son.

For a. while there was no change in the position of either the man or the woman. Then the woman swayed forward, and laid her face on the man's feet.

"Save him, save him, " she gasped.

Kellson stooped, lifted her from the ground, and placed her in the chair. He was struck by her extreme lightness.

"Rachel, " he said, "I never knew of this. What can I say to you now but, 'God help us both—or all three of us. ' I can give you no hope, but come and see me to-morrow morning at the Office. "

This seemed to comfort her. She stood up, faltered a "Good night, " and went out of the house with feeble steps.

Kellson sat down in his chair and thought. His brain was quite calm, and his mind was clear, He heard the rumble of the waggon, and the voice of the boy shouting to the bullocks as he drove the team. He stood up, and mechanically seized his hat and stick. He wondered where the keys of the Office were kept. He would go down to the Office, find the record, and strike the lashes out of the sentence. No—the sentence must stand. The one stainless record which his conscience held up to him, was that of his public life. He had never yet done a deed in his official capacity of which he was ashamed. He must not, at the close of his career, be guilty of a dishonourable action. The prisoner richly deserved his sentence. Let him undergo it.

"At the close of his career. " Yes, for Kellson felt that he could no longer live. His limit of endurance had been reached. Life had for some years past been a sore burthen, and now he could carry it no longer. Had he not longed for a child—for a son? Did he not know that such would have made his wife a happy woman and him a contented man? To live, to know of that degraded thing, for whose existence he was responsible, being there at the convict station amongst the other human animals, and becoming lower and more degraded every day. To look forward through two long years of misery and apprehension to the return of—his son. His son—a strange yearning towards the vicious creature he had carelessly glanced at that morning, took possession of him. He started up again, and seized his hat. He would go down, even though it were nearly midnight, and get the gaoler to admit him to the prisoner's cell. He made a few steps towards the door, and then stopped. No, better not. Reality would blast the delicate glamour-bloom with which his imagination had clothed for the moment that sordid form. It was the beauty of the eyes that haunted him. He knew that these imaginings were false. In another moment they were gone. What— after two years to meet that horrible cringing creature with the angel's eyes, in the street, and know him as his son—his son that he had asked God for in the days when he used to pray. Better a hundred deaths.

Suicide. Why not? Suicide was said to be disgraceful. Why? Other nations, more civilised in some respects than ours, had held it to be honourable. Not if one has responsibilities. His wife—well—he shrewdly suspected that she would be glad of her freedom. He had no child— —Oh, God! Yes he had.

Disgrace to his wife and to his other relations. Ah! here came in the beauty of his plan. Suicide would never be suspected.

Kellson went into the bedroom and opened his portmanteau. From the pocket of the partition he took a little bottle of chloral hydrate, a drug which he was in the habit of using when insomnia pressed heavily upon him, as it periodically did. The chloral was in five-grain tabloids. His usual dose was three tabloids or fifteen grains. He now counted twenty tabloids into a tumbler, which he half filled with water.

The front door was still open, and Kellson, remembering this, went to shut it. The moon had now soared high above the mountain, and a spectacle, wonderfully and wildly beautiful, was revealed. Kellson walked into the garden and gazed on it. The mist, no longer smooth and clinging, but drawn and curled into fantastic wreaths, was rising slowly into the windless sky. The tired-out man took one lingering look, and then walked quickly into the house. He locked the front door and went into the bedroom.

He undressed quietly and got into bed, after laying his clothes tidily on one of the chairs. The chloral had not yet quite melted, so he took his tooth-brush and stirred the contents of the tumbler with the handle. In a few moments the last tabloid had dissolved.

Kellson blew the candle out and took a sip of the chloral mixture. It was so strong that it made him cough. He lit the candle and added more water. It then struck him that the room might smell close when the people entered it on the morrow, so he got up and opened the window wide. He then returned to bed, drank off the contents of the tumbler, and lay down.

For one wild moment terror at the lowering face of Death took possession of his soul. It was as though he could see the awful features taking form out of the darkness. The dread destroyer that he had with daring hand roused unseasonably from his lair, seemed to fill the room—the house—the sky—and call him forth in tones of thunder to the black and freezing void. Light! Light!

He started up in bed and began to grope for the matchbox. But this passed away. The face of Death grew mild, and then seemed to smile. He lay down on his side, his face turned from the open window, composed himself into a comfortable attitude, and fell softly into the deepest of all sleeps.

THE QUEST OF THE COPPER.

"A beast with horns that rend and gore
My army rushes through the world;
The white plumes flutter in the fore,
Like mists before a tempest whirled;
The roaring sea when storms are strong
Is not so fierce, the lion's wrath
Is tame when swells the battle-song
That frights the clouds above my path!

"My beaten shields to thunder thrill,
My spears like lightning flash between,
Till raining blood their brightness kill,
Or dim to lurid red their sheen!
At morn and eve the splendid shine of burning clouds
I hail with joy—
The sky thus gives its son the sign
To rise up mighty, and destroy!"

                Zulu Pictures. Tshaka.

I.

TSHAKA, king of the Zulus, sat in state in his Royal Kraal one morning in the month of March, 1816. His throne was a log of white ironwood standing on its end, from the upper portion of which the stumps of three thick branches expanded, thus giving it the rough semblance of an arm-chair. The ends of the stumps were rounded and polished. The throne was standing upon the skin of a large, black-maned lion, and the king's feet were resting upon the mane. A number of indunas, councilors, and officers stood around the king in respectful attitudes, or moved about quietly, and silently.

Tshaka's mother, Mnande, sat on the ground some distance away, her ear strained to catch every word chat fell from her son's lips. A few yards behind her five young girls crouched on their knees and elbows, each with an earthen pot of beer, or a skin of curdled milk before her. As each new-comer arrived within a certain distance of the throne, he flung his spear and shield to the ground, and then came forward. When he reached within about twenty paces of Tshaka, he held his right hand high over his head and called out

"Bayete, " which is the Zulu royal salute. He then advanced and prostrated himself before the King's feet.

Tshaka was a man of magnificent build. He sat perfectly naked except for a bunch of leopard tails slung from his waist, and a few charms fastened to a thin cord around his neck.

Kondwana, commander of the 'Nyatele regiment, an induna of the Abambo tribe, was called before the king. He approached, under the customary obeisance, and then stood up.

"You will take, " said Tshaka, "what remains of the 'Nyatele regiment (a regiment that had suffered very severely in a recent campaign from fever in the coast swamps above St. Lucia Bay, as well as from slaughter by the spear), and go to the country beyond the mountains of the Amaswazi, where the green and yellow stones from which the red metal (copper) is smelted, are dug out of the ground. You will bring back so much of these stones as will cover, when heaped up, the skins of three large oxen. You will return before the Summer rains have fallen. Go. "

Kondwana was a distinguished man. He had, years previously, fought against Tshaka, but since his tribe, the Abambo, had made submission, and had been incorporated into the Zulu nation, he had served his new master with faithfulness and zeal. But one of the awkward conditions of savagery is this, that whenever a subordinate shows any extraordinary capacity, and consequently attains to a position of influence, his master is apt to regard him with jealousy and fear, and will therefore often destroy him ruthlessly on the first shadow of a pretext. In jealousy and mistrust of capable subordinates, the average savage potentate resembles Louis the Fourteenth of France, of pious memory, who could never bear to have a really capable man near his throne in a position of trust. Kondwana happened to be under the ban of Tshaka's suspicion, which, once roused, was never allayed. This is the explanation of his having been sent with his splendid regiment on a useless expedition through the deadly fever country just to the south of Delagoa Bay, between the Lebomba Mountains and the sea, and of his now having to go with the effective remnant of his veterans on a quest for copper to a hypothetical spot only vaguely rumoured of.

Amongst the spoil of a recent and very distant northern raid were a few copper bangles, and the prisoners from whom these were taken said that the metal had been smelted from green and yellow stones dug out of a mountain far to the north. In a native forge at one of the villages sacked, a few stones of the kind described had been found, and these were brought to Tshaka. No other information on the subject was to be had, yet Kondwana at once prepared to start upon his quest, knowing that if he failed to carry out the king's order to the very letter, his life would inevitably pay the forfeit.

Kondwana was a tall and very powerful man, jet black, but with a pleasing expression of countenance when not moved to wrath. He was as brave as a lion, and perfectly loyal to the king.

Tshaka possessed the faculty of inspiring loyalty to a high degree, but he was unaware of this. Being of a highly suspicious nature, he sacrificed to his groundless apprehensions numbers of his most loyal and devoted adherents.

Kondwana returned to his kraal after being shown specimens of the mineral which he had to seek. These were a few small lumps of shining stone—some being blue in colour and some yellow. In others both colours were present. When freshly broken, the blue specimens were beautifully iridescent, and showed tints such as are seen in the peacock's tail. Upon arriving at the headquarter military kraal next morning, he mustered his regiment, and found it to be about four hundred and fifty strong (effective). There were several hundred more at the kraal, but they were still suffering from fever. The men were all veterans, and thus wore head-rings, circular bands about seven inches in diameter, of a black substance composed principally of gum. These bands being about an inch thick, were fixed to the hair around the crown of the head, and thus afforded a very effective protection against blows.

The expedition started. A number of the men carried strong iron picks for the purpose of digging out the ore. They took a small herd of cattle for immediate use as food, but they depended upon proximate spoil for future sustenance. After crossing the Pongola river, the party made a detour inland so as to avoid a collision with the Amaswazi, with whom Kondwana did not want, just then, to fight. This took them through some very mountainous country, where they suffered grievously from cold. Some of the men in whose blood germs of fever still remained, began to sicken, and were mercifully put to death. But as it advanced through the mountains the little party had some very enjoyable fighting and looting, the

Mantatee tribelets offering no more resistance than afforded pleasant exercise. The loot was ample, and the soldiers simply feasted on meat. At night they often warmed themselves before the burning huts. They obtained from the vanquished Mantatees many soft, warm skins, for the mountain tribes, living under a comparatively cold climate, had become very expert in tanning. These skins were carried for them by the good-looking young women of the kraals which were "eaten up, " for the lives of such, when their services were required, were generally spared.

It was only the veterans of the Zulu army that wore head-rings, but there was one man with Kondwana's contingent whose head was ringless. This was Senzanga, the son of Kondwana's elder brother Kwasta. Senzanga had been spared by a fortunate accident when his father's kraal and its inhabitants had been destroyed a few months previously by Tshaka's order. Being fleet of foot, he had escaped to the bush, and he had ever since had a precarious existence as a fugitive, being fed by some women at the risk of their lives. Hearing through them of an expedition under the command of his uncle, he went, on ahead, and at the Pongola appeared and asked for Kondwana's protection, as well as for leave to accompany the expedition. Kondwana knew that he ran a serious risk in not killing Senzanga at once, but after consulting with his officers, he decided on venturing to spare the young man's life, meaning to deliver him as a prisoner to Tshaka on the return of the expedition, and then pray that he might be pardoned for the fault he had not committed, and which had been so heavily punished.

After getting well past the Amaswazi country, the expedition left the mountains, and traveled through the low, wooded plains that lie between the Drakensberg on the north-west, and the Lebomba hills on the south-east. In this region no men dwell: except the wretched "Balala, " naked and weaponless fugitives from the Tonga and other tribes, whose villages had been destroyed in war, and who had escaped to lead a life in the desert compared with which death by the spear would have been merciful.

The existence of the dreaded tsetse fly, whose bite is fatal to any domestic animal, accounted for the lack of human inhabitants. The cattle which Kondwana's men brought with them began to droop, and soon could proceed no further. After being bitten by the tsetse, animals gradually waste away, and sometimes live on for months, becoming more and more emaciated. If, however, rain happens to fall, they die off very quickly. The men set to work and killed all the remaining cattle. They ate what they could of the meat, loaded themselves and the captive women with as much of the remainder as could be carried, and then traveled as swiftly as they could in a north-easterly direction, towards the Limpopo river. Once across the Limpopo, they knew they could easily reach the Makalaka country, where, doubtless, loot abounded. They knew all about this from the Balala, whom they from time to time captured and questioned. None of these could, however, give any information as to where the copper ore had come from.

In the meantime, game was plentiful, although somewhat difficult to capture. Their most successful mode of hunting was this; —about a hundred men would lie in ambush in some place where, judging from the footmarks, wild animals were in the habit of passing. These men would take cover wherever they could, breaking off branches of trees for purposes of concealment where growing reeds, shrubs or grass did not suffice. They would lie or crouch about five yards from each other, in three lines about ten yards apart.

The remainder of the contingent would then divide into two parties, one of which would extend to the right and the other to the left, in open order, each party forming a long chain gradually stretching out. The leaders, after going out a certain distance, would curve inward towards each other until they met. A large area would thus be enclosed. As soon as the chains joined, by the leaders meeting, the grass was set alight, and immediately afterward smoke arose at numerous points around the enclosed space, whilst the men all rushed inwards towards the ambush. The terrified game, seeing themselves almost surrounded by a ring of fire, rushed madly to what seemed to them the only place at which they could possibly escape. When the herd reached the ambush, the men sprang to their feet, and dashed at it with their spears; the skirmishers, or as many as had been able to close in on the heels of the game, rushing in at the same time. It was their practice to avoid interfering with buffalo or other dangerous game so far as possible, but pallah, hartebeeste, koodoo, waterbuck and other antelopes were slain in the manner described, sometimes in great numbers. Then plenty would reign for a season.

These game-drives were fraught with considerable danger, and on several occasions some of the men in ambush were trampled to death or seriously hurt.

Every night the lions roared around their encampment, attracted by the smell of the meat, but repelled by the fires around which the men slept. It was found that so long as game was plentiful the lions did not come close enough to give any serious trouble—they could always he heard growling, but they made no attack—but in passing through regions where game was scarce, the lions, grown bold from hunger, would prowl round and round the camp, silently, and with deeply lurid eyes. One morning, just before dawn, a lioness dashed into the camp, seized a sleeping man by the shoulder, and began dragging him off. But in a moment the marauder was surrounded by spears, and then a desperate struggle took place. The night was dark, and the watch fires were nearly dead. Some of the men seized firebrands, which they held aloft so as to enable their comrades to see. The lioness died hard. The first frantic dash she made broke the ring for an instant, and she got two men down under her, one with a broken neck, and the other with a dislocated hip, whilst a third, who was dashed backwards by a blow from her paw, had his skull fractured and his shoulder broken. But Senzanga sprang on the lioness from behind, and by a lucky stroke plunged his spear into her spine just over the loins. The spear stuck fast between two of the vertebrae, and the animal gave a roar so tremendous, that it completely deafened for the moment those nearest to her. But she was now helpless, and so was easily dispatched. Day soon broke. The man with the dislocated hip was killed, the lioness was skinned and her meat eaten, and the expedition moved on, the men singing what is known as "the war-song of the lion, " in full chorus.

The Limpopo river was reached one evening after a hot, waterless march of over forty miles. The summer floods had subsided, and the lovely, forest-fringed stream, with crystal-clear currents swirling and eddying amongst the rocks, lay before them, full three hundred yards in width. The meat was nearly finished, the little remaining being putrid from the heat, but Kondwana rested his men for a couple of days amongst the shady trees on the bank. They knew that the Makalaka cattle were not far off, and a couple of days' hunger was, to Zulu soldiers, not very much of a hardship. On the morning of the third day after reaching the river, the expedition crossed. The crossing was not easy work, as many of the swirling channels were deep and rapid; moreover, on almost every rock crocodiles basked. But the men linked arms, four abreast, and dashed into the water singing their regimental war-song, and in spite of all difficulties reached the opposite bank without the loss of a man.

II.

A somewhat awkward circumstance was this; —a number of the men had lost their spears, and the loss of his weapon by a Zulu soldier was a crime admitting of no palliation or pardon. The Zulu soldier carried only one spear—a frightful weapon, with a broad blade and a short, thick handle. The use of this weapon (ikempe) had been introduced by Tshaka, who substituted it for the light throwing assegai (umkonto). Although quite discarded in war, the assegai was still used in the chase, and the men and boys were encouraged to keep up the practice of assegai throwing. Many of Kondwana's men had brought assegais with them; for the expedition not being a purely military one, discipline was not kept up so strictly as otherwise it would have been.

It was found, however, in hunting, that the light assegai was not effective in bringing down game. When used in stabbing, the weight was not sufficiently great, nor was the blade large enough to inflict a fatal wound; when hurled, the weapon was often lost through the animal escaping with it sticking fast, and being seen no more.

On some occasions the droves of game were so dense that no difficulty was experienced in killing animals by stabbing them at close quarters, but often such could not be done, only a few being driven into the ambush. Then the men had to choose between growing hunger and the risk of losing their spears through the wounded animals escaping, spears and all. As a matter of fact this had often happened, so much so, that by the time the expedition reached the Limpopo, nearly a fourth of the men were either weaponless, or else were armed only with light assegais.

After crossing the Limpopo, the expedition trended slightly to the westward, towards the hilly country where, according to the Balala, many of the cattle of the Makalakas were to be found. On the afternoon of the second day after crossing, troops of cattle and afterwards scattered villages were sighted. The alarm had evidently been given, for it could soon be seen that the cattle were being hurriedly driven off, and when the first village was reached, it was found to be deserted, However, by probing with their spears in the dung of the cattle kraal, the men easily found the flat stones covering the mouths of the underground corn-pits, and in these a fair supply of millet was found. So the men lit fires and cooked the grain. It was dark before they had finished eating, and then they built up the fires, piling on heavy logs which were lying near. Certain faint, twinkling lights were visible on a hillside very far off, and in the direction in which they had seen the cattle being driven in the afternoon, and towards these Kondwana led his men silently, and at a swinging trot.

About an hour before dawn the vanguard suddenly stopped, and the rest of the force formed up slowly in wings, as had been directed. The barking of dogs was heard some distance ahead. The Zulus were now in a comparatively open Country. A grassy expanse between two shallow, forest-filled valleys sloped up gently in front. Kondwana sent scouts ahead. These soon returned with the report that they had found a number of armed men sleeping around some huts close to a kraal which was filled with cattle. The dogs barked incessantly, out as much on account of the Makalaka strangers at the kraal as the Zulus. As a matter of fact, after the alarm was given late in the afternoon, as many of the Makalakas as could be communicated with had assembled here. Scouts had reported in the evening that the strangers were looting the corn from the pits, and only a couple of hours before Kondwana called a halt in the darkness, the fires that the Zulus had lighted were still to be seen burning brightly. Moreover, Kondwana had been very careful in preventing the huts being burnt, lest the Makalakas should infer that his force was moving on. By abstaining from burning the huts he completely deceived the Makalakas, who could not conceive it possible that a hostile force would pass a hut without setting it alight, so they slept in fancied security, little deeming what was in store for them.

Kondwana divided his force into three, each division numbering nearly a hundred men. These took up positions at equidistant points, lines connecting which would have formed an equilateral triangle, the little cluster of huts surrounded by the sleeping Makalakas being in the centre. The dogs, tired of barking at the different parties of Makalakas which had arrived during the night, did not make so much of a disturbance as might have been expected under the circumstances. The three divisions formed themselves into double lines, and then advanced slowly inwards until, at a signal from Kondwana, they yelled out the war cry and rushed forward. In a few minutes all was over. The unfortunate Makalakas were an easy prey; they hardly attempted to resist, but rushed from one side to the other, vainly attempting to escape from the ring of spears. By sheer weight of numbers, they at length broke through on the one side, and then about half of them escaped to the forest. They left over two hundred bodies on the field. The Zulus did not lose a man.

Some women and children rushed out of the huts. Most of them were slain, but some few were taken prisoners. Morning soon broke, and showed the dead lying in every direction, and the ground strewn with weapons which had been cast away in the rout. A few copper ornaments were found upon some of the women, who, upon being questioned, pointed to the north and said that the metal had been brought from there long ago.

The kraal was found to be full of cattle, some of which were at once slaughtered and eaten. Shortly after sunrise, a party of about a hundred Makalakas approached to within a short distance of the huts. When they caught sight of the dead bodies they turned and fled, body pursued by the Zulus for a short distance. None were, however, caught. Kondwana had again given the strictest orders that no huts were to be burnt, so as to avoid spreading the alarm to a distance, for as long a time as possible.

Next morning, large bodies of Makalakas appeared on the surrounding hills, but they were evidently afraid to come near. About midday three men approached to within hailing distance, and asked that three of the Zulus might come out for the purpose of parleying. So Kondwana and two of his men went out, and when they arrived within about a hundred yards of the others, stuck their spears into the ground and called out to the Makalakas to do the same, which they did. The two parties then met, and began to discuss matters.

The Makalaka spokesman inquired of Kondwana who he and the men were, and why they were making war on the Makalaka nation. Kondwana replied to the effect that he and his men were Zulus sent by Tshaka to obtain copper; that they did not want to make war, and had only done so because they found armed men assembled to oppose them.

It could at once be seen that the mere name of Tshaka made a considerable impression. The spokesman replied that the Makalakas did not want to fight with the Zulus, that the copper ore was found in the country of the Balotsi, to the northward, and that a party which the Makalaka chief had sent in the previous year for the purpose of fetching a supply of the ore, had never returned.

It was finally agreed that Kondwana's explanation should be communicated to the Makalaka Chief, and then the two parties separated, after arranging to meet again on the following day.

Next morning the three Makalakas returned, and the spokesman told Kondwana that guides would be provided by the Chief to lead the expedition to the place in the Balotsi country where the ore had been found, and that food for the use of the Zulus on the journey would be provided. All this was due to the fact that the terror of Tshaka's name had penetrated even thus far. Moreover, up to this, none of the Makalakas had come near enough to the main body of the Zulus to be able to see in what force the latter were, and those who had escaped from the slaughter of two nights previous, had greatly exaggerated the number of the assailants.

So on the following day, the Zulus started for the Balotsi country, under the guidance of five old Makalakas, who were stated to have accompanied a copper-seeking expedition many years back. A large herd of cattle, a few of which were pack oxen, had been sent down by the Chief. They loaded the pack oxen with their picks, and with the remainder of the millet which they found in the grain pits at the captured kraal.

The men who had lost their weapons re-armed themselves with the best of those of the slaughtered Makalakas. Such were, however, but poor substitutes for the terrible broad-bladed, thick-handled spears which had been lost, yet they were better than nothing.

The guides led Kondwana and his men through a part of the country which was very thinly populated, so they saw hardly any human beings and no cattle—nor were any signs of cultivation visible. They passed far to the eastward of the populated areas. One day two strange men joined the guides, and after traveling for a short time with the expedition, disappeared. This roused the suspicions of Kondwana, but the guides, although questioned apart from each other, each declared that the strangers were only casual travelers. As a matter of fact, these men were messengers laden with the doom of Kondwana and every man in his force.

This is what had happened. Until the Zulus started from the captured kraal, the Makalakas were under the impression that they had to deal with a full Zulu regiment, numbering probably two thousand men, but when the expedition moved off, and its numerical weakness thus became apparent, the Makalaka Chief at once determined on its destruction. So messengers were at once dispatched in every direction to collect the Makalaka forces, and the two "casual travelers" had been sent to tell the guides to desert two days after crossing the mountain range separating the Makalaka from the Balotsi territory, and, if possible, to take the cattle with them.

Weak as the Zulus were in point of numbers, the Makalakas did not yet dare to attack them.

The gigantic forms, the red shields and the gleaming, broad-bladed spears of Kondwana's small band, and the terrible evidence of prowess as shown in the night attack, had inspired great dread. Moreover, the Makalaka Chief determined on making sure that not a single man should escape to tell the tale to Tshaka. So as the Zulus marched on, a large army, collected from all available quarters, followed on their track at a respectful distance. Fleet runners had been sent on ahead to endeavour to arouse the Balotsi, and thus the Makalaka Chief trusted to being able to crush his foes as though between the jaws of a vice. The guides had been told to delay the march as much as possible by avoiding the direct route wherever such could be done without creating suspicion.

Kondwana and his men reached the mountain range which is a continuation of the great Quathlamba or Drakensberg chain, and saw great frowning precipices rise over steep slopes covered with dense forest. One long winding valley, overhung by precipitous cliffs, cleft the range, and through this the guides led them. At the head of the valley the range was slightly depressed, and a saddle was thus formed between two high peaks. Elevated tablelands, gently sloping to the north-west, and intersected by narrow, shallow valleys, stretched away from the level of the saddle. Each valley carried its stream of water, running between low banks covered with a thick growth of reeds. It was now May, and the cold at night on these high plains was very severe. Fuel was scarce, and the Zulus consequently suffered very much. They had now for some days been passing through a totally uninhabited country. Game was very plentiful, but impossible to capture in the open.

They pressed forward along an old disused foot-path, or rather a number of such, running parallel. As a matter of fact they were on the route which had been traversed lay the Makalaka expedition sent for copper ore in the previous year, and which had not returned nor been heard of.

On the morning of the third day after crossing the saddle, it was found that the guides and the cattle had disappeared during the night. Kondwana found that, overcome by fatigue, the two sentries had fallen asleep at their post, so he speared them with his own hand. He then called the men together, and they deliberated as to what course they should pursue. With one accord it was decided to go forward.

Taking up the track of the cattle, parties were sent out to endeavour to recover them, and between twenty and thirty head, which had become foot-sore and were thus unable to proceed, were brought back in the afternoon. These were at once killed, and the expedition moved on next morning, the men carrying the meat.

The men were now very footsore, in spite of the sandals which they had from time to time made out of the skins of the slaughtered cattle. They were gaunt and haggard from nearly three months of hardship and exposure. Their faces were sunk and their limbs emaciated. Yet no thought of returning before the object of the expedition should have been accomplished occurred to them.

Three days after that on which they had discovered the desertion of the guides, they began to pass human skeletons lying on the path, the bones scattered about and broken, evidently through the agency of beasts of prey. All those that had contained marrow had been cracked, apparently by the jaws of hyenas. Late in the afternoon they reached a spot where about forty or fifty disjointed skeletons were lying indiscriminately. Kondwana noticed scattered about, a quantity of mineral similar to the specimens shown to him at Tshaka's when he received his instructions. "Ah ha! " said he, "this accounts for their not having returned. "

The unfortunate copper-carriers had evidently been surprised, surrounded, and killed to a man—probably by the Balotsi. The Zulus, delighted at obtaining evidence of the bare existence of the thing they were seeking, walked about, picking up fragments of the ore, which they put into their skin wallets. It was evident that the greater part of the ore had been removed, yet every man of the expedition was able to secure a piece which he looked upon as a kind of amulet to bring him good fortune. There was a little fuel obtainable where they camped for the night, and the weary, haggard men went to sleep feeling in better spirits than for a long time past.

Just at daybreak next morning the sentries gave the alarm, and the Zulus sprang to their feet to find themselves surrounded by foes. A large Balotsi impi had been sent to intercept them.

The attack began at once, and for a time the struggle was fierce. But at close quarters one Zulu was a match for ten Balotsi, so the assailants were soon glad to retire, leaving nearly a hundred dead behind them. The Zulus lost about five or six men. It was broad daylight when the Balotsi drew off, and the Zulus could see their enemies massed round them in every direction, and outnumbering them excessively. Both parties paused for a time, each watching the other. The sun rose up over the mountains, the sky was clear as a dewdrop, and a bracing breeze swept down the valley, making music through the quivering reeds. Herds of eland, hartebeests, gnu, and other game, stood on the slopes afar off, and looked down on the dark masses of men standing still in grim silence after their desperate struggle.

Then Kondwana gave the order to retreat. There was no other course possible. Hardly any food was left, and the Balotsi were in such force as to render it impossible to cope with them successfully.

So the Zulus began to retire along the course by which they had advanced, and thus their travail entered into its final stage of long agony.

III

Back towards the saddle at the top of the pass through the mountain range marched Kondwana and the Zulus, the Balotsi force accompanying them at a respectful distance on each side. The Balotsi had had a severe lesson, and were not anxious to come again to close quarters. They found, moreover, that throwing the assegai was not of much avail on account of the large shields which the Zulus carried. Besides, the Zulus made a practice of picking up the assegais falling near or amongst them, and returning these, often with deadly effect, for, being physically much stronger than the Balotsi, their effective range with the assegai was correspondingly greater.

The Zulus stalked on in grim silence, the Balotsi shouting at them in an unknown tongue. At this stage the Balotsi had no intention of attacking.

They knew, what the Zulus did not know, that the Makalaka impi was waiting just on the other side of the saddle. They, the Balotsi, would just keep the Zulus in view, and then assist in their annihilation after the Makalakas had tamed them somewhat. So the Balotsi gave way consistently whenever the weary and footsore Zulus showed a disposition to charge.

The Zulus had thus little save hunger to fear so long as they were in the open country. They marched on, breaking into a trot whenever their course led downhill, during the whole of the day on which their retreat began. Each man still had a small supply of meat left, and portions of this they ate raw as they proceeded. At dusk the foremost of the Balotsi were some distance behind, and after marching for about two hours longer the weary fugitives lay down and rested. Sentries, which were relieved after very short watches, kept guard all night. Before daylight next morning they again started, and the previous day's average of speed was kept up until sundown, when they reached the saddle. They had seen nothing of the Balotsi all day. In fact the latter were a fair day's march behind.

Kondwana halted his men on the north-western side of the saddle, and then went forward with another man for the purpose of reconnoitering. When he looked down the valley, what he saw caused even his brave heart to sink. About a mile from him was massed the advance division of the Makalaka army, and as far as he could see beyond, the smoke was arising from numberless fires.

Kondwana returned to his men, and then the situation was discussed. The majority were in favour of making a dash down the valley and cutting a road through their foes. But the young man Senzanga made a suggestion which soon met with general approval.

All had seen that the Makalaka guides had not led them by a direct route from the captured kraal to the pass, but had made a considerable detour to the eastward. The object of this was now apparent. Senzanga's suggestion was to the effect that they should avoid the pass, striking boldly through the mountains to the south-west, trusting to being able to force their way through the forest on the coast side of the range. They could then make direct for some point on the Limpopo, higher up than where they had crossed. By going straight, they could reach the river by a much shorter journey than the previous one. Senzanga's plan was adopted, so after a cheerless rest of a few hours they started, working slowly up a long spur to the westward of the high peak flanking the saddle on the right-hand side.

As a matter of fact, the Zulus, by their extraordinarily rapid march, had reached the saddle exactly twenty-four hours before their arrival was thought possible by the Makalakas. The fact that the Zulus had begun to retreat had been signaled back by means of fires along the mountain tops, but they were not expected to be seen for another two days. When the Balotsi next day reached the saddle, expecting to find that the Zulus had been already slaughtered, they found, to their astonishment, that nothing had been seen of the fugitives. But the mystery was soon solved—the trail was found leading up the spur, and the intention of the Zulus became immediately clear to the Makalaka Chief, It was now his turn to be seriously alarmed, for if these men should succeed in reaching Zululand, an impi of Tshaka's terrible destroyers would soon be on its way to wreak vengeance. Therefore, at any cost, the fugitives must be intercepted and destroyed to a man. So the Makalakas hastened down the pass, after instructing the Balotsi to keep on the trail of the Zulus over the mountains, harass their rear, and notify their whereabouts by lighting fires on the nearest hills surrounding them every night. But this was a service for which the Balotsi had no stomach. They were a long way from home, and were almost without food; they had tasted of the Zulu spear, and it was bitter. So after making a pretence of obeying, they turned round and hurried homeward as fast as they could.

Kondwana and his force found the mountain range to be less formidable than they had anticipated, but nevertheless their sufferings were awful. Food, they now had none, and hunger gnawed at them with incessant and increasing violence. Their feet were so sore that every step over the rough, stony ground caused torture. Every now and then men dropped, unable to proceed further, and were at once speared by their companions.

On the evening of the day after they had struck into the mountains, the Zulus reached the forest-belt on the coast slope, and in front of them, distant about two days' easy march, could be seen the shining, wood-fringed reaches of the Limpopo, beyond which lay their only chance of salvation. But between them and the Limpopo was the Makalaka army.

That night the Zulus lay close to the upper margin of the forest, keeping neither watch nor ward. When the darkness set in, they could see below them the watch-fires of their foes, and they were thus able to tell approximately where the Makalakas were in greatest force.

It now became quite apparent to Kondwana that there was still a slender chance of escape if the men could only hold on a little longer without food. The left wing of the Makalaka army was slightly to the left of the Zulus, and if the latter could only manage to trend off a little more to the right, and find a passage through the forest, they might be able to creep past the Makalakas and even reach the river before being overtaken. As a matter of fact, the Makalaka Chief had again underestimated the marching capacity of the Zulus, and had not come far enough along the foot of the mountain range to the south-west, to intercept them.

Kondwana expounded his view of the situation to the men, who were almost in despair, and then called for volunteers to cross a valley and ascend a spur to the left, and there kindle fires. This spur was almost in front of the main division of the Makalaka army. Ten men volunteered for this service, and returned late in the night, after having performed it effectively.

Towards morning the Zulus again moved on, bearing down cautiously through the forest to their right. The Makalakas thought that Kondwana's fires were signals from the Balotsi to indicate that the fugitives were in the forest below the spur. They never supposed that the Zulus would indicate their whereabouts by lighting fires. So when daylight came, the Zulus had succeeded in outflanking their foes, and were making, as fast as starvation and their lacerated feet would let them, for the river.

Towards noon, a herd of cattle was seen. This was at once taken possession of, and soon a number of the beasts were slaughtered. The starving men tore the raw, smoking flesh, and drank the blood greedily. They then cut up the hides and bound pieces around their feet. After this, and a short rest, they felt like new beings. Hope took the place of the blank despair which had overwhelmed them a few hours previously. Another effort and they would reach the river beyond which lay safety. So they started again, driving the remainder of the herd of cattle before them, and each man carrying a small quantity of meat. Their number was now reduced to but a little over two hundred.

But they were not to escape from the toils. Their trail had been discovered, and the pick of the Makalaka impi was now overhauling them fast. Yet they had another short respite. It seemed indeed as if Fate were playing with them. They traveled on through the night, and in the darkness the pursuers lost their trail.

The Makalakas thought that the Zulus would make for the river at its nearest point, losing sight of the fact that the latter were strangers, blindly groping in unfamiliar surroundings; so when morning broke, the pursuers found that the trail was lost. They soon, however, ascertained that they were proceeding by a course parallel to that taken by the fugitives, and about a mile to the right of the latter. In spite of all they had under-gone, the Zulus were still keeping the lead slightly, but their limit of endurance had almost been reached. They were now making down a long, gentle slope towards the river, which was only about four miles distant. They had abandoned the cattle, and their formation was lost; in fact, they were just a disorganised mob of staggering men. The Makalakas were now gaining on them rapidly. The foremost of the pursuers did not make direct for the Zulus, but for a point lying between the latter and the river, so as to intercept them.

When Kondwana saw that they were cut off, he called out his men to halt, so they formed up and then lay down on the ground to rest. On came the main body of the Makalaka impi, and soon the haggard little band of Zulus was surrounded by foes outnumbering them by more than ten to one. At a signal from Kondwana, his men sprang to their feet, and forming themselves into a ring, faced the enemy on all sides. Under the stimulus of attack they almost ceased to feel fatigue. They knew they had now to die, and they burned with fierce resentment against the foes that had so pitilessly tormented them.

Kondwana gave the order that they were still to make for the river — now only a few hundred yards distant, keeping, as far as possible, their circular formation. The circle was formed two deep, the men of the outer ring sloping their shields outwards and those on the inner ring sloping their shields inwards, so as to ward off the assegais passing over the opposite edges of the circle. The Makalakas came on, making a horrible noise in which a buzzing sound seemed to mingle with a rumble formed in the throat. In the meantime reinforcements to the Makalakas came pouring in, and massing principally between the Zulus and the river, for the Chief had impressed on all the necessity for not allowing a single Zulu to escape.

The slaughter began with a discharge of assegais from all sides at once, the Zulus crouched down, covering as much as possible of their bodies with the shield. A few men fell, but the gaps were at once filled by the circle shortening in. For some time the Zulus only resisted passively, the circle slowly moving on towards the forest-fringe of the river, and consequently the Makalakas became bolder, and closed in nearer and nearer to the doomed circle. But the Zulus did not mean to die quietly. All at once they stopped in their slow, silent progress, and the Makalakas moved in closer, thinking that the time for finishing them off had arrived. Then the war-cry rang out, and with one splendid dash the Zulus were amongst the densest mass of their foes. Nothing could withstand the fury of their onslaught and the Makalakas fell under their spears like corn to the sickle.

The sun was just sinking. The Zulus had broken almost completely through the thickest portion of the ring formed by their foes. Only a few yards before them was the dense river-forest, offering sanctuary. But escape was not to be.

Having been unable to re-form after the charge, they were practically defenceless against a tremendous attach on their rear led by the Makalaka Chief in person, whilst hundreds of assegais were hurled in with deadly effect from both sides. About twenty bleeding men managed to reach the forest, but their pursuers leached it at the same time, and one by one the Zulus died in desperate hand to hand encounters amidst the twilight of the trees.

As night fell, the Makalakas drew off under the impression that the last Zulu was dead. Their own loss had been heavy. In the final charge they had been cut down by wholesale. But the Chief now felt safe from the avenging wrath of Tshaka.

Three of the Zulus were, however, still alive. Kondwana the induna, Senzanga—the man without a head-ring, and one other, had fallen into an old elephant-pit, the surface of which was completely covered over with brushwood. Dry leaves and twigs had accumulated at the bottom, and thus the shock of their fall had been lessened. Wounded and bleeding, they lay in the pit until the howling of the hyaenas told them that the Makalakas had withdrawn from the field of battle.

Of the four hundred veterans who had, but a few months previously, departed on the quest of the copper, only these three remained. All the splendid valour displayed, all the incomparable devotion and endurance manifested, had been wasted—poured out like their blood on the sand— sacrificed to the senseless suspicions of a brutal, irresponsible tyrant.

Nor was any living creature one whit the gainer—save the hyaenas.

IV.

Tshaka, King of the Zulus, sat in his royal kraal one morning in November, 1816. His Majesty was in a bad temper. Umziligazi and his clan, the Amandabele, rather than stay and all be killed on account of a misunderstanding over some loot, had arisen and fled across the Drakensberg to such a distance, that pursuit—for the present, at all events—was out of the question. Other things, worries from which the most despotic a ad irresponsible monarchs are not free, were also annoying him. Consequently those to whom he had lately been granting audience had had a bad time of it. In fact the executioners were busy every day.

One of the chief indunas ventured to communicate the fact that a very old and strange-looking man, who did not appear to be quite right in his wits, together with a. slightly younger, though equally weird-looking companion, craved an audience with the king.

Tshaka shared to the fullest extent those superstitions which form such a salient characteristic of all the Bantu tribes. Now, all savages believe that persons whose wits are affected are wizards, whom it is good policy to propitiate, and whom he may be dangerous to offend. Therefore the king signified that the strangers might approach.

Two men were then led before Tshaka. They were both fearfully emaciated and gaunt, and were scarred from head to foot. The elder man could not walk alone, bur leant upon the shoulder of the younger as he hobbled along, using the remains of a broken spear, the blade of which was worn down to a knob, and the shattered handle of which was bound together with little thongs—as a walking stick. This man (the elder) had the appearance of great age. His form was bent, and the little hair which he still retained was quite white. His battered head-ring, being attached only by one side, shook as if it would fall off on account of the motion caused by his walking. He appeared to be nearly blind. At the entrance to the Royal Kraal he had been ordered, according to established rule, to give up his spear, but he resisted so energetically that they allowed him to retain it— and, after all, it could hardly be called a weapon. He carried a small skin wallet slung to his waist.

The younger man looked old with the oldness that comes not of time but of suffering. His very flesh seemed to have disappeared, and his eyes had sunk deep into his head.

Kondwana, and Senzanga had travailed heavily since we left them on the night after the slaughter, in the elephant-pit on the northern bank of the Limpopo. After resting in the pit for a short time, the three survivors crept out and tried to cross the river. Kondwana and Senzanga succeeded after grievous pains, but the other man, who was desperately wounded, was swept away in one of the swirls and drowned.

For months that seemed to them like long-drawn years, Kondwana and his companion crept slowly southward, subsisting on whatever they could pick up in the way of food. Gum, exuding from the acacias, wild fruits, birds' eggs, young, nestling birds and honey, formed their principal fare. "Incinci, " the honey-bird, was their best friend and purveyor, and often led them to where the bees had stored their treasure in hollow trees, and holes in the donga-banks.

The wild beasts of the desert gazed at them without dread. Great troops of elephants went trumpeting past, taking no more notice of them than of the monkeys in the trees. Lions, hyaenas, and jackals came up and sniffed at them where they lay at night, and then passed on seeking daintier food.

They reached the land of the Amaswazi, and superstitious dread caused them to be assisted with food and shelter. They came to their own country and wandered on, unrecognised by those who had known them well less than nine months previously. And now they crouched to the ground at Tshaka's feet.

When they, with difficulty, arose after the obeisance, a change seemed to have come over Kondwana's face. The presence of the King, and the sound of his voice seemed to act as a stimulant upon the old man's torpid mind. In fact, they brought the farther past into stronger relief than the more recent, and then reality dawned up through the mists of fantasy that had clouded his brain for so long. His eye brightened. He remembered the past. He knew clearly where he was, and why he was there.

Gazing fixedly at the King, Kondwana let the broken spear fall to the ground, and then with his shaking right hand began fumbling at the skin wallet. After some little delay, he succeeded in opening this, and then he drew from it a lump of bright copper ore, about the size of a hen's egg. This he silently held out to Tshaka.

The King took the lump and examined it, and then looked sharply at the giver's face for a few seconds. Then in a tone of irritated surprise, he asked:

"Are you Kondwana?"

"Yes, my King."

"Where are your soldiers, and where are the stones you were sent to fetch?"

"The soldiers are dead, my King. Only this one and I are living. We were overcome by the Makalakas and the Balotsi. We slew them in crowds, but they were too many for us, and we had no food. I have brought the stone to show that I tried to do your bidding."

When Tshaka recognised Kondwana, his superstitious fears at once vanished. Here was no wizard potent for evil, but his own man Kondwana, the induna, whom he hated and had sent away so as to be rid of him. Besides, Kondwana stood there self-convicted of the deadly sin which admitted of no pardon; he had returned unsuccessful from an expedition; he had been defeated. Moreover, Tshaka was in a bad temper owing to the causes we have specified.

So he signed to one of his ever-ready executioners and said:

"Take them away and kill them."

The executioners approached, but Kondwana drew himself up with ineffable dignity, signed to them with his hand to pause, and spake in a firm voice.

"O King, for my own death I thank you, for why should I longer live? But this man is still young, and has done no evil deed. Let him wash his spear once in the blood of your enemies, and die at the tip of your battle-horn."

Tshaka, thoroughly enraged, was a fearsome sight. Like Peter the Great, his features worked and twitched horribly. Those who beheld him thus, felt that they were before the very face of Death, embodied and visible.

All in his presence, except the two doomed men, crouched to the ground and hid their faces in their hands. Even his mother, 'Mnande, more privileged than others, and often bolder in interfering in his counsels, bent down where she was sitting until her forehead touched the ground.

He glared speechlessly at Kondwana and Senzanga, who, having gone far beyond the limit of experience where Fear dwells, looked back quietly at his face. When he at length found his voice, it came in the semblance of a gasping roar:

"Take them away—Dogs."

Like men released from a spell, the executioners sprang on Kondwana and Senzanga and dragged them away, two men seizing each of them—one by each arm. Kondwana was unable to walk, so was dragged along the ground towards the place of execution, which was at the back of the Royal Kraal. When they had got out of the King's sight, even the executioners were moved to pity, so they lifted him on to the shoulders, and thus carried him to the shambles.

When Kondwana reached the place of execution, Senzanga was already dead, his neck broken by his head having been twisted round from the back, the usual mode of dispatch. They set Kondwana down on the ground, and then one of the executioners seized his head and twisted it; but it seemed as if on account of the tendons being so relaxed from emaciation, the spine would not dislocate, although twisted beyond the usual dislocation point, so the executioner sprang up, and seizing a club, crushed the skull in with one blow.

So Kondwana, even at the very last, tasted more than his proper share of the bitterness of death.

GHAMBA.

"That darksome cave they enter, where they find
That cursed man, low sitting on the ground,
Musing full sadly in his sullein mind."

FAERIE QUEENE.

I

WHEN Corporal Francis Dollond and Trooper James Franks of the Natal Mounted Police, overstayed their ten days' leave of absence from the camp on the Upper Tugela, in the early part of 1883, everybody was much surprised; they being two of the best conducted and most methodical men in the force. But the weeks and then the months went by without anything whatever being heard of them, so they were officially recorded as deserters. Nevertheless, none of their comrades really believed that these men had deserted; each one felt there was something mysterious about the circumstance of their disappearance. They had applied for leave for the alleged purpose of visiting Pietermaritzburg. They started on foot, stating their intention of walking to Estcourt, hiring horses from natives there, and proceeding on horseback. They had evidently never reached Estcourt, as nothing could be heard of them at that village. They were both young men—colonists by birth. Dollond had an especially youthful appearance. Franks was older. He had joined the force later in life. He and Dollond, who had only very recently before his disappearance been promoted, were chums.

Some months later in the same year, when Troopers George Langley and Hiram Whitson also applied for ten days' leave of absence—likewise to proceed to Pietermaritzburg—the leave was granted; but the officer in charge of the detachment laughingly remarked that he hoped they were not going to follow Dollond and Franks.

Now, neither Langley nor Whitson had the remotest idea of visiting Pietermaritzburg. It is necessary, of course, for the reader to know where they did intend going to, and how the intention arose; but before doing this we must deal with some antecedent circumstances.

Langley was certainly the most boyish-looking man in the force. He had a perfectly smooth face, ruddy complexion, and fair hair. He was of middle height, and was rather inclined to stoutness. He was so fond of talking that his comrades nicknamed him "magpie. " A colonist by birth, he could speak the Kafir language like a native.

Whitson was a sallow-faced, spare-built man of short stature, with dark brown beard and hair, and piercing black eyes. His age was about forty. He had a wiry and terrier-like appearance. A "down-East" Yankey, he had spent some years in Mexico, and then drifted to South Africa during the war-period which, it will be remembered, lasted from 1877 to 1882. He had served in the Zulu war as a noncommissioned officer in one of the irregular cavalry corps, with some credit. The fact of his being a man of extremely few words was enough to account for the friendship which existed between him and the garrulous Langley. Whitson was known to be a dead shot with the revolver.

This is how they came to apply for leave. One day Langley was strolling about just outside the lines looking for somebody to talk to, when he noticed an apparently very old native man sitting on an ant-heap, and regarding him somewhat intently. This old native had been several times seen in the vicinity of the camp, but he never seemed to speak to any one, and he looked so harmless that the police did not even trouble to ask him for the written pass which all natives are obliged by law to carry when they move about the country. The old man saluted Langley and asked in his own language for a pipeful of tobacco. Langley always carried some loose leaves broken up in his pocket, so he at once pulled some of these out and half filled the claw-like hand outstretched to receive them. The old native was voluble in thanks. There was a large ant-heap close to the one on which he had been sitting, and on which he reseated himself whilst filling his pipe. Against this Langley leant and took a good look at his companion. The man had a most extraordinary face. His lower jaw and cheek-bones were largely developed, but Langley hardly noticed this, so struck was he with the strange formation of the upper jaw. That portion of the superior maxillary bone which lies between the sockets of the eye-teeth protruded, with the sockets, to a remarkable degree, and instead of being curved, appeared to be quite straight. The incisor teeth were very large and white, but it was the development of the eye-teeth that was most startling. These, besides being very massive, were produced below the level of the incisors to a depth of nearly a quarter of an inch. They distinctly suggested to Langley the tusks of a baboon.

As is very unusual with natives, the man was perfectly bald. His back was bent, and his limbs were somewhat shrunken, but he did not appear in the least degree decrepit. His eyelids were very red, and his eyes, though dim, had a deep and intent look. Ugly as was the man—or perhaps by virtue of his ugliness—he exercised a strange fascination over Langley.

The old man, whose name turned out to be Ghamba, proved himself a talker after Langley's own heart. They discussed all sorts of things. Ghamba startled his hearer by his breadth of experience and his shrewdness. He said he was a "Hlubi" Kafir from Qumbu in the territory of Griqualand East, but that he had for some time past been living in Basutoland, which is situated just behind the frowning wall of the Drakensberg, to the south-west of where they were speaking, and not twenty miles distant.

They talked until it was time for Langley to return to camp. He was so pleased at the entertainment afforded by Ghamba, that all the tobacco he had with him found its way into the claw-like hand of that strange-looking man of many experiences and quaint ideas. So Langley asked him to come to the ant-heap again on the following day, and have another talk at the same hour. This, Ghamba, with a wide and prolonged exposure of his teeth, readily agreed to do.

Langley was extremely voluble to Whitson that night over his new acquaintance. Whitson listened with his usual impassiveness, and then asked Langley how it was that "an old loafing nigger, " as he expressed it, had impressed him so remarkably. Langley replied that he did not quite know, but he thought the effect was largely due to the man's teeth. But all the same he was "a very entertaining old buffer. "

Next afternoon, Langley was so impatient to resume conversation with his new friend, that he repaired to the ant-heap quite half-an-hour before the appointed time. He had not, however, long to wait, as Ghamba soon appeared emerging from a donga a couple of hundred yards away.

Langley was more impressed than ever. Ghamba told him all about the Basutos, amongst whom he had lived; about the old days in Natal, before even the Dutch occupation, when Tshaka's impis wiped whole tribes out of existence; of the recent wars in Zululand and the Cape Colony, and as to the probability of future disturbances. Charmed as was Langley by the old man's conversation, he felt that on this occasion there was a little too much of it, that Ghamba was not nearly so good a listener as he had been on the previous day, so when the latter at length put a question to him, thus affording an opportunity for the exercise of his own pent-up loquacity, Langley felt elated, more especially as several inquiries were grouped together in the one asking, Ghamba asked whether anything had been heard of Umhlonhlo; whether the capture of that fugitive rebel was considered likely, and whether it was true that a reward of 1500 pounds had been offered by the Government for his capture, dead or alive.

Umhlonhlo, it will be remembered, was the Pondomise chief who rebelled in 1880, treacherously murdered Mr. Hope, the magistrate of Qumbu, and his two companions, and who has since been an outlaw with a price on his head.

Langley replied to the effect that it was quite true such a reward had been offered; that nothing as yet had been ascertained as to Umhlonhlo's whereabouts, but that the Government believed him to be in Pondoland; that he was sure to be captured eventually; that he, Langley, only wished he knew where Umhlonhlo was, so as to have the chance of making five hundred pounds with which to buy a certain nice little farm he knew of; and that should he ever succeed in obtaining the reward and consequently taking his discharge and purchasing the farm, he would be jolly glad if old Ghamba would come and live with him. This is only some of what he said; when Langley's tongue got into motion, he seemed to have some difficulty in stopping it.

However, he paused at last, and then Ghamba, looking very intently at him, said;

"Look here, can you keep a secret? "

Here was a mystery.

"Rather, " said Langley.

"Will you swear by the name of God that you will not reveal what I tell you? "

Langley swore.

Ghamba drew near until his teeth were within a few inches of Langley's cheek, and said in a whisper;

"I know where Umhlonhlo is."

Langley started, and said in an awed voice;

"Where is he?"

"Wait a bit," said Ghamba, "perhaps I will tell you, and perhaps I won't. I like you, you have given me tobacco, and you are not too proud to come and talk to a poor old man. Now, you say you would like to make five hundred pounds and buy a farm?"

"Rather."

"And that you would let me go and live on the farm with you and end my days in peace?"

"I would, gladly."

"Well then, if I lake you to where Umhlonhlo is, and you kill him and get the money, will you give me twenty-five pounds, and let me keep a few goats, and grow a few mealies on your land?"

"I should think I would. But how could one man take or kill Umhlonhlo? They say he is well armed and that he has a lot of followers with him."

"Umhlonhlo," said Ghamba, glancing anxiously round as if he feared the very ant-heap were listening, "is hiding in a cave in the mountains, not three days' walk from here. He has not got a single man with him, because he fears being given up. He is really in hiding from his own followers now. My sister is one of his wives, and that is how I know all about it. I passed the cave where he lives, four nights ago, and saw him sitting by the fire. He has only a few women with him."

"And how do you think I should take him?"

"Take him? you should kill him. I will guide you to the cave by night, and then you can shoot him as he sits by the fire."

Langley, although no coward, was not particularly brave. He did not much relish the idea of alone tackling the redoubtable Umhlonhlo, a savage of muscle, who was reported to be always armed to the teeth. Moreover, he had no gun, and was but an indifferent shot with a revolver. So he thought over the matter for a few moments and then said:

"Look here, Ghamba. I do not care to tackle this job alone, but if I can take another man with me, I am on. "

"Then you will only get half of the five hundred pounds, and will not be able to buy the farm. You need not be afraid; you can shoot him without his seeing you. "

"No, " said Langley after a pause. "I will not go alone, but if you will let me take another man with me, it can be managed. It will make no difference to you; you will get your twenty-five pounds. "

"And how about my going to live on the farm with you? "

"Well, I could not buy the farm for two hundred and fifty pounds. Come, we will give you fifty pounds instead of twenty-five. "

Ghamba thought for a while and then said;

"Very well, I consent. But there need be only one other man, and you will write down on a piece of paper that you will give me the fifty pounds. When can we start? "

"I must speak to the other man, and then we wilt apply for leave. We had better start soon, or else Umhlonhlo may have gone to some other place of hiding. "

"Yes, we must lose no time. "

"All right, meet me here tomorrow and I will bring my friend. We will then settle all about it. "

"You must not mention this matter to any one else, and you must make your friend promise to keep the secret. "

"Oh, that's all right, " said Langley; "meet me here to-morrow just after dinner. "

Langley went back to camp, Ghamba looking after his retreating figure with a smile that revealed his teeth in a very striking manner. Langley was intensely excited, and exacted (quite unnecessarily) the most solemn promises from Whitson not to divulge the great secret which he confided to him. Whitson agreed at once to join in the enterprise, which was one after his own heart.

Next day the three met at the big ant-heap, and Whitson was very much impressed by Ghamba's teeth. He told Langley afterwards that they reminded him of a picture of the Devil which he had seen in a copy of the "Pilgrim's Progress." The old man's story appeared, however, consistent enough, in spite of his peculiar dentition.

So after a short conversation Langley and Whitson returned to camp, having made an appointment to meet Ghamba again on the following morning at sunrise, so as to finally arrange as to time of starting, &c. They went at once to the officer in charge of the detachment and applied for ten days' leave of absence for the purpose of proceeding to Pietermaritzburg, which was at once granted.

Next morning they met Ghamba again, and agreed to start on their expedition that evening. He explained that they must do all their traveling by night, and lie by during the day, because it would never do for him, Ghamba, to run the risk of being recognised by persons whom they might meet. For the sake of his Hlubi relations who were living amongst the Pondomise at Qumbu, it was absolutely necessary that he should not appear in the transaction at all. Were it ever to be even suspected that he had betrayed the Chief, not alone would he be certainly killed, but all his relations would be shunned by the other natives. He was an old man, so for him, personally, nothing mattered very much, but a man is bound to consider the interests of his family. Traveling only by night, and lying still and hidden during the day, were therefore absolutely necessary stipulations, and Langley and Whitson agreed to them as intelligible and reasonable. All being settled, the latter started for the Camp, Ghamba baring his teeth excessively as they walked away.

II.

At dusk on the evening of the same day, Langley and Whitson met Ghamba once more at the large ant-heap, and the three at once proceeded on their course. The only arms taken were revolvers of the Government regulation pattern (breech loading, central-fire). They carried provisions calculated to last eight days, but took no blankets on account of having to travel at night. When Ghamba volunteered to relieve them of a considerable share of their respective loads, Langley and Whitson were filled with grateful surprise.

The plan was as follows:

Whitson was to shoot Umhlonhlo, and then remain in the cave whilst Langley returned to the Camp to report what had been done, and cause persons who could identify the body to be sent for. They seem to have had no scruples as to the deed they meant to do; certainly Umhlonhlo deserved no more mercy than a beast of prey, nor does it seem to have struck them that possibly they might shoot the wrong man. But there was an air of conviction about the manner in which Ghamba showed his teeth when asked whether he was positive as to the identity of the man in the cave, that would have dissipated the doubts of most men. Besides this, he drew out the written undertaking which they had delivered to him, and said, with a profoundly business-like look:

"Do I not want the money? Should I take all this trouble if I did not know what I were doing? "

They walked all night, only resting once or twice for a few minutes. It was found that Ghamba; in spite of his age, was an extremely good walker; and when they halted at daylight, Langley was so done up that he could not have held out for another half-hour. Whitson, the wiry, had not yet felt the least fatigue.

This march had taken them to the very foot of the great Drakensberg range, and they rested in a valley between two of its main spurs. Here they remained all day, comfortably located in a sheltered nook, where there was plenty of dry grass. Their resting place was encircled by immense rocks. Although the surrounding country was desolate to a degree, and neither a human being nor an animal was to be seen, Ghamba would not hear of their lighting a fire nor leaving the spot where they rested. The weather was clear, and neither too warm nor too cold. They slept at intervals during the day, and at evening felt quite recovered from their fatigue. At nightfall they again started, their course leading steeply up the gorge in which they had rested. Although the pathway became more and more indistinct, Ghamba appeared never to be at a loss. Langley several times shuddered, when they passed by the very edge of some immense precipice, or clambered along some steep mountain side, where a false step would have meant destruction. He began to show signs of fatigue soon after midnight, so at Ghamba's suggestion a considerable portion of his load was transferred to the shoulders of Whitson, who seemed to be as tireless as Ghamba himself.

At daybreak they halted in the depths of another tremendous gorge with precipitous sides. The scenery in this particular area of the Drakensberg range, the neighbourhood of the Mont aux Sources, is indescribably grand and impressive, and is quite unlike anything else in South Africa. Enormous and fantastically-shaped mountains are here huddled together indiscriminately, and between them wind and double deep gloomy gorges, along the bottoms of which mighty boulders are thickly strewn. On dizzy ledge and steep slope dense thickets of wild bamboo grow, and a few stunted trees fill some of the less deep clefts, wherever the sunshine can penetrate. Splendid as is the scenery, its gloom, its stillness, its naked crags and peaks, its dark depths that seem to cleave to the very vitals of the earth, become so oppressive, that after a few days spent amongst them, the traveler is filled with repulsion and almost horror. Few living things have their home here. You might meet an occasional "klipspringer" (an antelope in habits and appearance somewhat like the chamois), a wandering troop of baboons, and now and then a herd of eland in the more grassy areas. There are said to be a few Bushmen still haunting the caves, but they are seldom or never seen.

In the afternoon, the sun shone into the gorge in which the travelers were resting, and for a few hours the heat was very oppressive. Whitson examined his revolver, removing the cartridges and replacing them by others. He then lay down to sleep, asking Langley to remain awake and keep a lookout. He had a vague feeling of uneasiness which he could not overcome. Langley promised to keep awake, but he was too tired to do so. He sat with his back against a rock, and after some futile efforts to keep his eyes open, fell fast asleep. By and by Ghamba woke him gently, and, pointing to Whitson, whose revolver lay in the leather case close to his hand, whispered;

"Did he not tell you to keep awake?"

Langley was grateful for this evidence of consideration, but he could not quite make out how Ghamba had been able to understand what Whitson had said. However, when the latter awoke, Langley said nothing to him about having disobeyed instructions.

Ghamba said that about two hours' walk would now bring them to Umhlonhlo's cave, so they started off briskly at dusk. Their course now led for some distance along a mountain ledge covered with wild bamboo, through which the pathway wound. Then they crossed a sleep saddle between two enormous peaks, after which they plunged into another deep and winding gorge. This they followed until they reached a part where it was so narrow that the sides seemed almost to touch over their heads. Beyond, the cliffs fell apart, and then apparently curved towards each other again, thus forming an immense amphitheatre. At the entrance to this Ghamba stopped, and said in a whisper that they were now close to the cave.

They now held a consultation, in terms of which it was decided that Ghamba should go forward and reconnoiter. So Whitson and Langley sat down close together and waited, conversing in low tones.

Whitson felt very uneasy, but Langley tried to argue him out of his fears. The more Whitson saw of Ghamba, the more he disliked and distrusted him and his teeth. The instinct which detects danger in the absence of any apparent evidence of its existence is a faculty developed in some men by an adventurous life. This faculty Whitson possessed in a high degree.

"Did you keep awake all the time I slept this afternoon? " he asked.

Langley feared Whitson, and felt inclined to lie, but something impelled him, almost against his will, to speak the truth now.

"No, " he replied, "I slept for a few minutes. "

Whitson drew his revolver and opened the breech.

"By God! " he said, "the cartridges are gone. "

Langley took his weapon out of the leather case and opened it. He found the cartridges were there right enough.

"Have you any spare cartridges?" asked Whitson.

Whitson had already loaded his revolver with the five cartridges which he had removed in the afternoon, but he again took these out and replaced them in his waistcoat pocket, and then he re-loaded with some which Langley passed over to him with a trembling hand.

"Look here," he said in a hoarse whisper, "we are in a trap of some kind. When that old scoundrel comes back, do not let him know that we have found out anything. We will walk on with him for a short distance, at all events, and then be guided by circumstances. Stand by when you see me collar him, and slip a sack over his head."

"Can we not go back now?" said Langley.

"Certainly not; we would never find our way at night. I guess we must see this circus out. If you have to shoot, aim low."

In a few minutes Ghamba returned.

"Come on," he said. "He is sitting at the fire in front of the cave. I have just seen him."

"Where is the cave," asked Whitson, "is it far from here?"

"We will reach it very soon; you can see the light of the fire from a few paces ahead."

They walked on for about fifty yards and there, sure enough, over a rocky slope to their left, and at the foot of a crag about three hundred yards away, could be seen the bright and fitful glow from a fire which was hidden from their view by a low ridge of piled-up rocks.

Whitson stood still and questioned Ghamba:

"Now tell me," he asked through Langley as interpreter, "how are we to approach?"

"The pathway leads up on the left side," replied Ghamba; "we will walk close up to the crag where there is a narrow passage between it and that big black rock which you see against the light. You two can lead, and I will tie close behind. I have just seen him. He is sitting at the fire, eating, and only the women are with him."

The last words were hardly out of the speaker's mouth before Whitson had seized him by the throat with a vice-like grasp.

"Seize his hands and hold them, " he hissed to Langley.

Ghamba struggled desperately, but could not release himself. Whitson compressed his throat until he became unconscious, and then gagged him with a pocket-handkerchief. Ghamba's hands were then tied tightly behind his back with another pocket-handkerchief, and his feet were firmly secured with a belt. An empty sack (from which they had removed their provisions) was then drawn over his head and shoulders, and secured round the waist.

"Come on now, quickly, " whispered Whitson, and he and Langley started off in the direction of the fire, after first taking off their boots.

They did not approach by the course which Ghamba had indicated, but made their way quietly up the slope straight against the face of the crag. They reached the heap of rocks, and crept in amongst them by means of another narrow passage, close to the inner end of which the fire was, and this is what they saw through the twigs of a scrubby bush which effectually concealed them.

A large cave opened into the side of the mountain, and just before the mouth was an open space about twenty yards in diameter, surrounded on all sides except that of the mountain itself by a wall of loosely-piled rocks, through which passages led out in different directions. Just in front of the cave burned a bright fire, around which crouched four most hideous and filthy-looking old bags, and against which were propped several large earthenware pots of native make, full of water. Standing behind rocks, one at each side of the inner entrance to the passage, which was evidently that communicating with the pathway indicated by Ghamba as the one they were to approach by, were two powerful-looking men, stark-naked, and as black as ebony, their skins shining in the light of the fire. Each man held a coiled thong in his hands, after the manner of a sailor about to heave a line. Whilst they were looking, a woman somewhat younger in appearance than any of those who sat by the fire, came out of the cave carrying a strong club about three feet long. She crouched down close to the man standing on the left-hand side of the passage, who, as well as his companion, stood as still as a marble statue, and in an expectant attitude.

Whitson and Langley, with their revolvers drawn, suddenly stepped out of their concealment, and walked towards the fire. This evidently disconcerted the men with the thongs, who apparently did not expect their intended prey to approach by any course except the passage near which they were standing; but after a slight pause of hesitancy, the thongs were whirling in the air, and descending, lasso-fashion, upon the shoulders of the intruders. The noose caught Langley over his arms, which were instantly drawn close against his body as the throng tightened, so he was thus rendered completely powerless; but Whitson sprang, quick as lightning, to one side, and escaped. Three shots from his revolver rang out in as many seconds, and the two men and the woman—who was in the act of lifting her club to brain Langley—lay rolling on the ground, each with a bullet through the head.

The four old hags at the fire began to mow and scream, and got up and hobbled into the cave. Whitson drew his knife, and cut the thong with which Langley was vainly struggling, and then the two men, pale as death, looked silently at each other with starting eyes.

Whitson re-loaded his revolver, and then made a sort of torch out of dry reeds; a pile of which lay close at hand. He then, leaving Langley to guard the cave, carefully examined all the passages and spaces between the rocks, but he could mid no trace of any one. The two men thereupon entered the cave, Whitson holding the torch high over his head. They found that it ran straight in or about fifteen paces, and then curved sharply to the left.

It was about four paces in width, and about eight feet high—the roof being roughly arched. The walls and roof were covered with thick, black, greasy soot; and an indescribably horrible stench, which increased the further they advanced, made them almost vomit. They found that where the cave curved to the left, it ended in a circular chamber about eight paces in diameter, and at one side of this crouched the four old hags, huddled together, and mowing and chattering horribly.

Across a cleft about two feet wide, in the right-hand wall of the cave, a stick was fixed transversely, and hanging to this were some lumps of half-dried and smoked flesh. Whitson went up close and examined these carefully. He drew back with a shudder, and his face changed from pale to ashen grey.

He and Langley then went outside and stood for a while in the fresh air. They could endure, just then, no more of the foetid atmosphere inside. After a short time, they gathered up some dry twigs and reeds, and set several little heaps alight at different spots inside. This had the effect of making the atmosphere more bearable in the course of a few minutes. They then made a larger fire in the middle of the cave, and proceeded to examine it more closely.

They found several old iron picks, such as are used by natives in cultivating their fields, some very filthy skins, a number of earthenware pots, a few knives, and an axe; but nothing more.

The floor of the cave was of clay, and at one spot it appeared to have been recently disturbed. Here Langley began to dig with a pick, which, just below the surface, struck against some hard substance. This, when uncovered, proved to be a bone. He threw it to one aide and dug deeper, uncovering move bones, some old, and others comparatively fresh, but emitting a horrible smell. He stooped and picked one up, but dropped it immediately, as if it burnt him. It was the lower jawbone of a human being.

"Great God! " he gasped. "What is the meaning of this? "

"It means, " said Whitson, "that we are in a nest of bloody cannibals."

Langley dropped like a stone, in a dead taint; so Whitson dragged him outside, and leaving him to recover in the open air, returned to the cave, He then seized the pick and began digging, unearthing some new horror at every stroke. A glittering object caught his eye; he picked this up and found it to be the steel buckle of a woman's belt. He glanced towards the cleft in the rock where the lumps of flesh were hanging, and caught his breath short. Going outside he made another torch which he lit, and then he returned and carefully examined, the loosened surface. Another glittering object caught his eye. This, when examined proved to be an old silver watch, the appearance of which seemed familiar. He forced open the case, and saw, roughly scratched on the inside, the letter D. He now recognised it; he remembered having once fixed a glass in this very watch for Dolland, about a month before the latter's disappearance. Continuing his search "Whitson found the iron heel-plate of a boot, and a small bunch of keys.

Whitson drew his revolver, and picking up the torch went into the terminal chamber. Four shots fired in quick succession reverberated immediately afterwards through the cavern.

Whitson then went outside to Langley, whom he found sitting down near the fire, looking, if possible, more ghastly than before. The presence of Whitson seemed, however, to act on him as a kind of tonic, and he soon pulled himself together sufficiently to assist in piling a quantity of fuel upon the already sinking fire, which soon blazed brightly, lighting up the mouth of the cavern and the space in front of it. One of the bodies of the men who had been shot was lying on its side, with the face towards the fire. Whitson examined the mouth, pushing back the upper lip with a piece of stick. He found that the shape of the mouth and the development of the teeth were the same as Ghamba's. The other bodies were lying on their faces, so he did not trouble to examine them.

Whitson then told Langley to follow him, and the two walked down the footpath towards where they had left Ghamba, Him they found lying motionless in the position in which he had been left about an hour previously. They removed the sack and the gag and untied his feet, first taking the precaution to fasten the belt by one end of his bound hands, Whitson holding the other. They then signed to him to proceed towards the cave, and this he silently did without making any resistance. He looked calmly at the three dead bodies, but said not a word. Langley held him, whilst Whitson again tied his feet together with the belt, and then they placed him with his back against a rock, facing the fire which was still blazing brightly.

His lips were drawn back in a ghastly, mirthless grin, and the tusks were revealed from point to insertion, Langley questioned Ghamba, but he would not speak. After several attempts to force him to answer had been vainly made, Whitson said—

"Now tell him that if he speaks and tells the whole truth, he will only be shot, but if he does not speak, he will be burnt alive. "

This was interpreted, but the threat had no apparent effect. So Whitson seized Ghamba and dragged him to the fire, where he flung him down on the very edge of the glowing embers.

"Now, " said Whitson, holding him down with his foot, so that he got severely scorched, "for the last time, will you speak? "

"Take me away from the fire, and I will speak," said Ghamba, in English.

So they lifted him, and set him again with his back to the rock.

"Now," said Whitson, "go ahead, and no nonsense."

"If I tell the whole truth," said Ghamba, still speaking English, and with a fair accent, "will you swear not to burn me, but to shoot me, so that I shall die at once?"

"I will," said Whitson.

"You too must swear," said Ghamba, looking at Langley.

"Yes, I swear."

"Very well," said Ghamba, "I will tell you everything, but you must both remember what you have sworn to."

"Yes, all right," said Whitson. Ghamba then looked at Langley, who repeated the words.

"I will tell you," said Ghamba, "all I can remember, and you can ask questions, which I shall answer truly. You have heard of Umdava, who used to eat men in Natal long ago, after the wars of Tshaka — well, he was my uncle. After Umdava had been killed and his people scattered, my father, with a few followers, came to live amongst these mountains. But we found that after having eaten human flesh we could enjoy no other food, so we caught people and ate them. These two men lying dead are my sons, and that woman is my daughter. My four wives were here to-night. They are very old women. Have you not seen them?" he asked, looking at Whitson.

"They are in there; I shot them," said Whitson, pointing to the cave.

"I had other children," continued Ghamba, quite unmoved, "but we ate them when food was scarce."

"Have you always lived, all these years, on human flesh?" asked Whitson.

"No, not always; but whenever we could obtain it we did so. There is other food in these mountains. Honey, ants' eggs, roots, and fruit; besides game, which is, however, not very easy to catch. But we have often all had to go away and work when times have been bad. Besides, I have a herd of cattle at a Basuto kraal, and I have been in the habit of taking some of these now and then, and exchanging them for corn, which the women then went to fetch. But we have always tried to get people to eat, because we could enjoy no other kind of food. Sometimes we got them easily; and when we were very fortunate we used to dry part of the meat by hanging it up and lighting a fire underneath, with green wood, so as to make plenty of smoke."

"Have you killed many white people?" asked Whitson.

"Yes, a good number; but not, of course, as many as black. Lately we have always tried to catch whites, because when you have eaten while flesh for some time, the flesh of a native no longer satisfies you."

"Why not?"

"The flavour is not so strong."

"Did you induce the other two policemen to come up by means of the story about Umhlonhlo?"

"Yes, they came up just as you did, and my sons caught them with the thongs. Umhlonhlo has brought us plenty of food."

"Were you able to take the cartridges out of their revolvers as you did out of mine?"

"No, I had no opportunity; but it was not necessary, because my sons were so expert at throwing the thongs that they could always catch people over the arms, and thus render them unable to shoot."

"How did they manage to become so expert?"

"By continued practice, I used to walk up the path over and over again, and let them throw the thong over me. Then the woman was always there with the club, so that if one of the thongs missed, she was ready to strike. I, also, was usually ready to help in case of necessity. "

"Why did you think it necessary to take the cartridges out of my revolver? "

"Because I feared you from the first, and were it not that he, " baring his teeth, and glancing at Langley, who shuddered, "looked so nice, and that we wanted fresh meat so badly, I would not have risked bringing you. But it would have been all right if I had only let your revolver alone. "

"You say Umhlonhlo has brought you plenty of food; did you ever get any one besides ourselves and the other two policemen to come up here by telling them that story? "

"Yes, two others—one a man who was searching for gold on the Free State side of the mountains, and the other a trader whom I met at Maseru. But these each came alone. "

"I see the buckle of a woman's belt in there! Whom did that belong to? You surely never got a white woman up here? "

"Yes, we did, " said Ghamba, with a horrible half smile which bared the gums high above the sockets of his tusks. "She was a young girl who strayed from a waggon passing over the mountain by the Ladysmith road, only a day's walk from here. I pretended to show her the shortest way to her waggon, and thus brought her as far as she could walk in this direction. I then killed her, and came up here and fetched my sons. We carried her up in the night. She was very young and plump, and I have never eaten anything that I enjoyed so much. " (Whitson turned cold with horror. He remembered the girl's mysterious disappearance, and the fruitless searches undertaken in consequence.) "His flesh" (glancing again at Langley) "looks something like hers did, and I am sure it would taste just as nice. There was still a little of her left when I went away last week. If you will go in there and look where the rock is split on the right-hand side, you will——" But he did not finish the sentence, for a bullet from Whitson's revolver crashed through his brain, and he tumbled forward on his face into the fire.

It was only after tremendous difficulty that Whitson and Langley succeeded in escaping from the mountains. However, on the evening of the third day after their adventure in the cave, they came in sight of the police camp, Whitson sat down on a stone, and motioned his companion to do the same.

"See here, Sonny, " he said, "I want to have a short talk with you. I am a bit cross with you as the cause of my having been sucked in by that damned, murdering old walrus. You ought to know the inhabitants of this country better than a simple stranger like me, and so I took your lead. Now, another thing, you nearly bust us both by your blasted foolishness in going to sleep that day; but let that pass, because perhaps it would have been worse if we had not been put on our guard; not but that it would take a damned smart cannibal to eat Hiram Whitson. But this is what I am coming to: you my boy are a darned sight too fond of hearing your own tongue clack. Now, lake a warning from me, and don't let a word of what has happened since we left Camp—for Pietermaritzburg— pass your lips. I did all the shooting, and I'm not a bit ashamed of it; but, by the eternal God, if you open your lips to a soul, I'll shoot you like a dog or a cannibal. Remember that, Sonny, and say it quietly over to yourself the first time you fee that you want to blab. Now shake hands. "

This was probably the longest speech that Whitson had ever made.

About two years after the events narrated, Whitson took his discharge and returned to America. He left behind him a sealed packet addressed to his Commanding Officer, and which was not to be delivered for twelve months after his departure.

Owing, however, to a strange combination of fortuitous circumstances, this packet never reached its proper destination; its wrapper, bearing the address, having been scorched off in a fire which took place in the house where it was left.

NOTE.

Many people have heard or read of the cannibals of Natal, who turned large tracts of country into a shambles in the early part of this century, after Tshaka's impis had swept off all the cattle, and then kept the miserable people continually on the move, so that they were unable to cultivate. One Umdava originated the practice of eating human flesh. Gathering together the fragments of four scattered tribes, he trained them to hunt human beings as others hunted game. This gang was a greater scourge to the country surrounding the present site of Pietermaritzburg than even Tshaka's murdering hordes. It was broken up in or about the year 1824 when the Europeans first came to the country, and the remnants of many scattered tribes returned and settled under their protection.

All this is history with which most people in South Africa are familiar, but many do not know that some of the cannibals fled to Basutoland where, amongst almost inaccessible mountains, they carried on their horrible practices for many years.

It is a well-known fact that when men once surrender themselves to any unnatural and brutal vice, the gratification of the abnormal instinct thus acquired becomes the most imperative need of their nature. The Falkland Islands case, as bearing specially upon the foregoing narrative, may be mentioned. Some convicts escaped from the Falkland Islands convict station, and succeeded in reaching the coast of Patagonia. They then endeavoured to make their way to Monte Video, but, having to keep along the shore so as to avoid the natives who would have killed them had they ventured inland, were easily intercepted by the Government cutter which was always dispatched in cases of the kind to head off fugitives upon their only possible course. Of the party, only one man was found alive. In their dreadful need the men had cast lots as to who should be killed and eaten by the others, and this went on until only the one man remained. His sufferings had been so horrible that he was let off any further punishment, and simply brought back to the Island to complete the term of his sentence. Some months after, this man induced another to escape with him in a boat, and when the boat was overtaken it was found he had killed his companion for the purpose of eating the latter's flesh. This was apparent from the fact that the supply of food which the fugitives had taken with them was not exhausted.

UKUSHWAMA.

"No ghosts, they say.
What is a ghost? —
Nay, what are thoughts and stars and winds?
They cannot tell — they show at most
Those formal swathes the pedant binds
Across clear eyes, the while he plugs
The apertures of liberal lugs."

SHAGBAG on Dogmatism.

I.

I had been for two days endeavouring to frame a workable quarantine scheme in respect of an outbreak of lung sickness amongst the natives' cattle in several of those deep valleys which cleave the Xomlenzi range from the Northern bank of the Tina River, and it was late in afternoon when I reached the kraal of my friend Numjala, Headman over a section of the Baca tribe of Kafirs. The mounted policeman who had accompanied me let his tired horse fall in a particularly bad drift, thus laming the animal, and had had to remain behind in consequence. Thus I was alone, but this circumstance did not trouble me, because my horse was fresh, and I knew the country well.

Numjala is a roan of parts; he must be well over sixty years of age, but his eye is bright and his wit is keen. He is well off, for a native, and very hospitable.

The moon being new, her pale crescent sank quickly after the sun, but the sky was perfectly clear and the stars more than ordinarily bright. To reach home I had about twelve miles to ride, that is, by taking a short cut along footpaths; along the main road the distance was nearer twenty.

Numjala was very anxious that I should spend the night at his kraal, and offered, would I agree to remain, to kill a juicy looking kid and roast it for supper. I had, however, promised my wife to return by midnight, and I feared she might be uneasy were I not to do so; I therefore declined the invitation.

"Does your horse lead well?" asked Numjala.

"Not particularly," I replied; "why do you ask?"

"You say you are going by the footpath past the Ghoda bush?"

"Yes."

"Unless your horse leads well, you will never get him past the Ghoda to-night, this being the night of the New Moon. You will certainly never ride him past."

The Ghoda bush is a narrow strip of forest running down the side of a steep mountain which forms one side of a valley, the other side being formed of a perpendicular cliff, at the foot of which a stream brawls. The strip of forest does not quite reach the stream, a grassy glade, about twenty-five yards in width, lying between. Over this glade the footpath leads. The Ghoda is about a mile from Numjala's kraal, and just beyond it is the drift over the stream.

"What has the Moon to do with it?" I asked.

"That is a hard question. I only know that no horse can be ridden past the Ghoda after sundown when the Moon is new."

"Look here, Numjala," I said reprovingly, "a man of your intelligence ought to be ashamed of even pretending to believe such a thing. Why this is worse than what you told me about the grass not growing at the spot where Ncapayi and his men were killed by the Pondos."

"Is it?"

(Ncapayi, Great Chief of the Baca tribe, with many hundreds of his followers, was killed in 1845 in a battle fought with the Pondos on the Northern bank of the Umzimvubo river, between what is now Mount Frere and the sea.)

"Yes, and nearly as bad as your account of the snow falling on Tshaka's impi and killing hundreds of his soldiers, whilst it fell nowhere else in the neighbourhood."

"Why should not that be true?"

Fearing that it would be useless to attempt demonstrating to Numjala that, logically, no one is bound to prove a negative, I evaded his question, and said:

"You told me the other day that you believed in witchcraft. Surely you did not mean that?"

"Why not? Did not your great Prophet—every one of whose sayings all you white people believe so thoroughly and follow so carefully"—it will be seen that Numjala can be sarcastic—"believe in evil spirits, and even drive them forth? Is it not this that the witch-doctor claims to do? Did not the Prophet of the Wesleyans believe in witchcraft? Now, if you believe the words of your Prophets about some things, why not about others?"

I was surprised at these words, knowing Numjala to be a heathen, and I suppose I must have shown this, for he added:

"I have talked with the missionaries, or rather they have talked to me. Besides, my brother's son is an evangelist, and he has told me a lot about what is taught in the schools."

"But, surely, Numjala, your experience must have taught you that witchcraft is all humbug (imfeketu), and that before the English rule, the witch-doctor was simply the instrument of the chief for suppressing people who became too rich or too powerful."

"The witch-doctor may often be a humbug (kohlisi), and yet it is possible that there may be such a thing as witchcraft. A missionary, to whom I pointed out that some who preached the gospel had been since proved evil men, once said much the same thing to me about religion. I am an old man, and I have learnt many things, and one is this: He who always says of the thing he does not understand, 'This cannot be,' is in danger of being put to shame."

"Well, Numjala, tell me the story about the Ghoda bush, for I am sure there is a story."

"I will tell it if you stay here to-night."

"But I must go home."

"Well then, I will make a bargain with you. You have already passed the Ghoda, and therefore you know the footpath leading to the drift."

"Yes, I know it well. I traveled it only the day before yesterday."

"Very well. You will take the pathway tonight, and if you can ride your horse past the Ghoda, well and good—you will go home to your wife. If not, you will return and sleep here. The kid will be roasted, and you shall hear the story. Do you agree?"

"Certainly I do."

"Just one thing:—remember that you are to ride past. It is possible, although I think it unlikely, that you might reach the drift if you blind-folded the horse and led him."

"I quite understand. Good-bye."

"I will not say 'Good-bye.' You will return and hear the story."

As I rode away laughing, I heard Numjala calling out to his son Tantiso, telling him to catch a certain kid, kill it, and prepare it for immediate roasting. My course led down the hillside, and then along the level bottom of the valley on the left-hand side of which is the Ghoda Bush. The stream was on my right, and the pathway on which I was riding ran parallel with it, distant about twenty yards.

As I drew near the Ghoda I felt somewhat creepy. My horse was a steady old stager, not at all given to shying. He went along at a quick amble, and as I neared the fateful spot, I freshened up my courage with the thought that in a few moments I would have crossed the drift, and then the Ghoda and its ghost would be well behind me. My horse was stepping out briskly and without showing the least sign of suspicion, when all at once he gave a loud snort and wheeled sharply to the right, completely unseating me, However, I did not fall off, as I managed to clutch hold of his mane. As I swung back into the saddle, I saw that we had narrowly escaped falling down the sleep bank into the stream.

To save my self-respect, I made another attempt to pass, but more or less the same thing happened, except that I kept my seat, and managed to avoid going so near the bank, I then left the horse to himself, and he ambled back to Numjala's kraal. When I dismounted he was wet with perspiration, and trembling violently. I will not say how I felt, but my sensations were not comfortable.

Numjala evinced no surprise, nor did he attempt to triumph over me in any way. Neither did he (then, or ever) ask me what had happened. He took my return, quite as a matter of course.

We sat down to supper. The kid was excellent, and the foaming koumis from the big calabash equal to champagne. After supper I spread my rug at one side of the fireplace—Numjala unrolled his mat at the other. We lay down and smoked our pipes in silence for some time, and then Numjala told me the following story.

II.

It is many years since I first came to live on this spot. I was then a poor man, although the 'great son' of my father, who was a chief of some importance. He died with Ncapayi in the battle on the Umzimvubo, and shortly afterwards all our cattle were swept off, I had then only two wives, and the eldest child by the first wife was a girl whom I called Nomalie. Many daughters have been borne to me since, and my kraal is full of their 'lobola' cattle, but the only girl of the lot that I was ever really fond of was Nomalie—perhaps because she was my first child.

"She grew up—tall and straight, with well-formed limbs. I remember that from her birth she had a soft look in her face, and her eyes were very large. She was rather light in colour. It was said that her mother's grandfather was a white man. Her mother's family came from the Amavangwane country, which is on the sea-coast, and I have been told that long ago a white man came out of the sea and took a woman of the tribe as his wife. One of this man's daughters was the mother of my wife, who was Nomalie's mother. It was strange that my wife showed no trace whatever of white descent, whilst Nomalie most certainly did, both in colour and feature.

"As soon as ever Nomalie reached a marriageable age, many men wanted to marry her, but when the suitors came to 'metja' (woo) she would have nothing to do with them. I soon found out the reason of this; she had grown fond of a young man named Xolilizwe, a son of the right-hand house of one of Ncapayi's counselors who, like me, had lost all his wealth. Xolilizwe dwelt with his uncle Kwababana—a very old man—over the hill at the back of the cliff facing the Ghoda. He was a few years older than Nomalie, and he often used to stay for weeks at a time here at my kraal. Xolilizwe was all that a young man should be, except that he was poor, and his uncle, old Kwababana, could give him nothing.

"Xolilizwe was brave and strong, and I had gladly given him Nomalie, but you know what we Kafirs are; no man will give his daughter to one who cannot pay 'ikazi' (dowry). Besides, no girl would want to marry such a man—no matter how much she liked him—for she would always be known as the woman for whom no dowry had been paid, and this would be a reproach to her and all her relations.

"Nomalie was very young, and I was so fond of her that I did not want to force her to marry against her will. But seeing how matters stood, I told Xolilizwe that he had better keep away. Shortly after this he disappeared from the neighbourhood.

"In the days I speak of, Lukwazi was the most important man in these parts. Although inferior to me in rank, he was very rich, and Makaula, Ncapayi's successor, had made him Chief over the people in this neighbourhood; consequently I was under him. Nearly all my father's people having been killed, the few who remained were placed under Lukwazi, his kraal was the one on the top of the second ridge beyond the Ghoda. No one liked Lukwazi, though many feared him on account of his cunning, and his wealth gave him power. He was a very big man, of a wrathful temper, and they said that though he loved the smell of other men's blood, he feared to smell his own. At the time I speak of he was an elderly man, and had (I think) twelve wives and many children.

"Well, one day Lukwazi called here in passing, and saw Nomalie. About a week afterwards two of his messengers came and said that he wanted her as his wife. I was both glad and sorry. Glad, because I was poor and wanted cattle, and when it is a question of lobola, a chief gives more than an ordinary man; but sorry because I disliked Lukwazi, and felt uneasy at giving him my favourite daughter. Of course I could not refuse, I being Lukwazi's man.

"Nomalie cried bitterly, and at first declared that she would never go to him, but I told her that she must, and that I would, if necessary, make her do so. I could not afford to fall out with Lukwazi, my Chief, and a powerful, revengeful man. Besides, the girl had to marry some one, and I naturally wanted her to marry him who would pay the most cattle. After a while she ceased to object, but she went about looking so sad that I never liked to see her. She used to come near me, and look into my face, and this made me feel so sorrowful that I tried to avoid her as much as possible. Just before they took her away I was so distressed at the sight of her misery that I could have even then put a stop to the marriage only that I was afraid to make an enemy of Lukwazi.

"At length they came to fetch her, and I shall never forget the look she gave me over her shoulder whilst being led away. Then I comforted myself with the thought that when she came back after the fifth day, driving the ox for the marriage feast, she would not look so miserable.

"In the middle of the second night after Nomalie had gone I was sleeping in my hut, and I heard some one trying to open the door. I asked, 'Who is there? ' and a voice (Nomalie's) replied, 'It is I, your child. ' I removed the door-pole, and Nomalie entered. I said, 'My child, what is this thing? ' but she did not speak. I threw some twigs on the embers, and when they blazed up, what I saw made me burn with wrath. The girl was naked, and her body and limbs were covered with wheals and scars where the women had beaten her because she would not allow Lukwazi to approach her.

"She sat down next to the fire and looked at me in silence until I could endure it no longer, so working up a semblance of anger to hide my pity, I said roughly, 'Why have you brought disgrace on your house, by leaving your husband? I shall send you back to-morrow! ' Instead of replying, she stood up, and taking my large spear from where it was sticking in the roof, she handed it to me. She then knelt down, and placing a hand upon each of her breasts, she drew them apart, and looked into my face. I knew she meant this to indicate that she wished me to drive the spear into her, rather than to send her back. To see if she were in earnest, I lifted the spear as if to strike, still keeping up the semblance of anger—but she just closed her eyes, smiled, and leant slightly towards me, I then saw she was in earnest, so I flung down the spear and said in a kinder voice that she should remain, and that Lukwazi might keep his cattle. When I had said this, she flung herself to the ground on her face, and wept as though she would die.

"Next day, Lukwazi's messengers came for Nomalie, but I told them they could not have her. Afterwards Lukwazi himself came with ten men armed, and said he would take his wife by force. I stood in front of the door of the hut, leaving Nomalie alone inside, and told Lukwazi that the girl refused to return to him, and that after the way she had been ill-treated, I should not force her to do so, Lukwazi said that the girl was now his wife, that he had married her with my consent, that he had now come to fetch her, and that he meant to have her. Just then I felt something put into my hand from behind, and when I closed my fingers on it I found this thing to be the handle of my big, broad-bladed spear. Then I heard the wicker door of the hut being closed, and the cross-bar being slipt into its place.

"Now when I realised what Nomalie had done thus silently, and other own accord, my heart filled with pride in my daughter, and I began to answer Lukwazi more boldly. I told him that I knew I had the law on my side—the girl had returned showing marks of ill-treatment, and I was therefore justified in keeping her—at all events until an inquiry had been held. Lukwazi said that, law or no law, he was going to take the girl away then and there, so I told him that I would slay with my spear the first man who tried to enter the hut. At this, Lukwazi and his followers became very wrathful, and I think they would have attacked me had it not been for what my daughter then did.

"Over the loud voices of the men we heard hers calling Lukwazi by name, and then all ceased speaking for the moment, Lukwazi replied to her, saying, 'What is it, my wife?'"

"The door of the hut is fast barred, and you cannot break it down so quickly but that I may set the hut in flames in several places before you enter. I will die in the fire rather than go with you."

"On hearing this, they all looked at one another, and shortly afterwards they moved off, Lukwazi still looking wrathful, and muttering fierce threats against me and my house.

"About a month afterwards Xolilizwe returned. He brought eight head of cattle which he had stolen from the Fingoes. He came here and asked me to give him Nomalie as his wife, offering the cattle he had stolen as an installment of the dowry, the balance of which he would pay later on, when able to do so. I consented, as I wanted to make up to the girl for any previous hardness, so she went as the wife of Xolilizwe to the kraal of his uncle, old Kwababana. There was not much of a marriage feast, for I still feared the anger of Lukwazi, and did not want to annoy him further. I warned Xolilizwe to be careful, as I felt sure Lukwazi would try and be revenged on some of us—and most probably on him through the witchdoctor. In fact I strongly advised him to take Nomalie away quietly, and go and dwell with our people on the Umzimkulu.

"It was early in summer when Nomalie went to dwell with Xolilizwe as his wife, and about three months before the feast of the first-fruits (Ukushwama). You know something about what then happens. Each chief sends away by night, and has a pumpkin, a mealie-cob, and a stick of 'imfe' (sweet-reed) stolen from the territory of some chief belonging to another tribe. These are mixed with medicines by the witch-doctor, and partaken of by the Chief and his family, in the calf-kraal before dawn on the morning of the day of the new moon. You have no doubt also heard that when a chief confers the honours of chieftainship upon his 'great son, ' who is to succeed him, a special Shwama is held, and that on such an occasion the stolen first-fruits have to be mixed, by the witch-doctor in the skull of a man who has been killed for the purpose. Many Europeans refuse to believe that this kind of thing still happens; nevertheless it does, and it will happen in spite of all the Government may do, so long as the Baca tribe is in existence. Even a Christian chief would require Ukushwama to be performed in respect of his son, or otherwise—as he well knows—the son would never be recognised as legitimately a chief.

"Now the skull used at Ukushwama must be that of a man of a certain rank, and is supposed to be that of an old man; but this is not absolutely indispensable. I have told you that Lukwazi, although a chief, was of low birth. Now, amongst the people in this neighbourhood were very few whose rank was even equal to his own, and therefore when it became known that at the next feast of first-fruits, his son Bobazayo was to take the great Shwama, people began to wonder whose skull would be required.

"I thought over the matter myself, and I found that the only three men about here whose skulls would do, were Kwababana— Xolilizwe's uncle— Xolilizwe, and myself. I at once made up my mind that Kwababana would be the man, because he was very old, and besides his rank was highest, his father having been the brother of Madikane.

"A short time before the feast, which begins with the new moon in the month which you call February, I went away to the 'great place' (residence of the paramount Chief of the tribe) intending to return in time for the opening ceremony.

"When I returned on the second-last day of the old moon, I was quite surprised to hear that Kwababana was quite well.

"As no one had heard of a killing, there was much speculation going on as to where a skull had been obtained; it being usual to kill for this purpose nearly a month before the feast—although this, again, is not a necessary condition.

"Well, we all assembled at Lukwazi's kraal on the last night of the old moon. I had not seen Xolilizwe since my return, and I was surprised at not finding him at Lukwazi's. Just before daylight the Shwama was administered to Bobazayo in the calf-kraal, and then to the members of his family. Upon two points I kept wondering: one was in connection with the skull—whose was it, and where had the witch-doctor obtained it? The other was the absence of Xolilizwe—where was he, and what excuse would he give for not being present when the great son of the Chief took the Shwama?

"We drank beer, and danced, and made merry all the forenoon. I saw a man near me who must have passed Kwababana's kraal in coming to the feast, and I asked him if he had seen anything of Xolilizwe. He told me he had heard that Xolilizwe was away following the spoor of old Kwababana's only milking cow, which had been stolen three days previously, and had not returned.

"Just after the sun had begun to fall, I saw my daughter Nomalie approaching. She walked in amongst the people and straight up to me without saying a word. I shall never forget her face—it was like the face of one that had been dead for several days—all except the eyes, which were full of fire. I knew at once that Xolilizwe was dead.

"She took my hand and silently drew me after her, and thus we walked down the footpath to the drift on the other side of the Ghoda, which you meant to have passed to-night. We crossed the stream, and she led me to the edge of the bush and pointed to something lying just inside the outer fringe of brushwood. I looked, and saw the headless body of Xolilizwe.

"I recognised the body at once. No other man that I knew hart such limbs as he. My unhappy daughter's husband had been slain by the thrust of a spear from behind through the left shoulder-blade. I tried to comfort Nomalie, and to get her to speak, but not a word passed her lips. After a while, she motioned me impatiently to leave her, so I went away, meaning to return later. I noticed a digging pick, and a stone nearly as large as my head, with a string of twisted bark tied around it, lying close to the body. I knew now in whose skull the first-fruits had been mixed.

"It was still early in the afternoon, so I went home. The day was hot, and I had drunk much beer, so I lay down and slept. I woke just at sundown, and went quickly down to the Ghoda, expecting to find my daughter there. But she was not to be found, neither was the body where I had seen it lying. Just afterwards, however, I found a heap of stones that appeared to have been just before piled over a mound of freshly turned earth. The pick was stuck into the soft ground next to it, so I inferred that Nomalie had buried the body of her husband and gone home.

"I went up to Kwababana's kraal, but Nomalie was not there. Old Kwababana was healthy in body for so old a man, but he was very childish, and just then the loss of his cow had quite upset him. He could tell me nothing about Nomalie, and when I told him that Xolilizwe was dead, he thought I meant the cow, and began to cry out. When I at last was able to make him understand that it was Xolilizwe I had said was dead, and not the cow, he appeared to be quite comforted, I then went back to my own kraal, but Nomalie was not there, nor had she been seen or heard of. So I ceased searching, thinking that she would be sure to return, sooner or later.

"Three days after, a little boy told me that something strange was lying in the pool just above the Ghoda drift. I went down at once to see what it was. The pool is quite shallow, it would hardly drown a man if he were to sit down in it. There I found my daughter's body, with the stone which I had seen lying near Xolilizwe's headless trunk tied to the neck by the string of twisted bark. It was a pity. She would have been the mother of men.

"I dug a hole where she had left the pick stuck in the ground, for I now understood she had meant the placing of the pick thus as a sign that she wished me to bury her next to Xolilizwe. Tomorrow, when you are going home, get off your horse and walk into the Ghoda bush at its lower extremity. You will see a large 'umgwenya' (kafir plum) tree just inside on your left, and underneath it two piles of stones. These are the graves. But my story is not yet finished.

"Lukwazi never saw another Shwama. The corn-yield that year was very plentiful, and in the early part of the winter beer flowed like water at every kraal. Lukwazi rode about with his followers from beer-drink to beer-drink, and he was drunk most of his days. On the evening of the fourth new moon after the feast of the first-fruits, Lukwazi and his men rode past here at full gallop. It was not yet dark. The sun had gone down and the moon was just disappearing. The party had been drinking beer for two days at the huts of Vudubele, the last kraal that you passed on your way here this afternoon, and all were mad drunk. They galloped down the valley, Lukwazi leading on a stout little grey stallion. He was beating his horse and yelling, and one blow made the horse swerve out of the path. There was an old ant-bear hole hidden in the grass, into which the horse trod, and falling, rolled over on its rider. Lukwazi lay quite still. His neck was broken.

"Since then, no horse will ever pass the Ghoda bush between sunset and sunrise when the Moon is new. "

Next morning I dismounted at the Ghoda, and walked into the forest. I found the large umgwenya tree without any difficulty, and underneath it were the two piles of stones close together. They were much overgrown with ferns and creepers. A large bush-buck leaped up and crashed through the undergrowth. His doe followed immediately afterwards, passing so close that I could see the dew-drops glistening on her red, dappled flank.

Kafir Stories

UMTAGATI.

"The great witch-doctor has come, and all
Sit trembling with cold and fear
As they list to the words from his lips that fall, —
The words all shrink to hear.
Lo! look at the seer as he whirls and leaps
The awestruck circle within,
Where each one shudders, and silence keeps
As he thinks of the untold sin.

"On his head is a cap of dark brown hair, —
The skin of a bear-baboon,
And the tigers' teeth on his throat, else bare,
Jangle a horrible tune;
The serpents' skins and the jackals' tails,
Hang full around his hips,
And a living snake from his girdle trails,
And around each bare limb slips."

The Witch-Doctor.

I.

THE motive and controlling factors of great issues are not always recognised by those most interested, neither does honour nor yet reward always fall to those who best deserve or earn them. In proof of the foregoing propositions the following narrative is adduced.

Teddy's full name was Edmund Mortimer Morton. He was a Government official holding the appointment of clerk to the Resident Magistrate of Mount Loch, which district, as everybody knows, is situated in the territory of Bantuland East, and just on the border of Pondoland.

Vooda was a native Police Constable attached to the Mount Loch establishment.

Teddy's age was twenty-six, but he looked several years younger. He was a pleasant-looking little chap, about five feet four inches in height, slightly built, with blue eyes, yellow hair and an incipient moustache upon which he bestowed a great deal of attention. His hobby was popular chemistry. This he indulged in, greatly to the entertainment of his friends and the detriment of his hands, which were generally discoloured in a manner that defied soap. He lived in a little hut just outside the village. This hut consisted of one room, and was shaped like a round pagoda. It had a pointed roof and projecting eaves made of Tambookie grass. The walls were of sod-work, plastered over and white-washed. Here Teddy dwelt—taking his meals elsewhere—and experimented in parlour-magic to his heart's content.

Vooda was a constable. He was a short, stout man, with a deep, although not wide knowledge of human nature; not wide only for lack of experience. He had dwelt all his life amongst the natives surrounding Mount Loch, and he could read them like so many books of Standard I. He could, moreover, tell by looking at a witness in court, whether that witness were speaking truth or lying, and the magistrate recognised and utilised this faculty. Vooda and Teddy were great friends, Vooda taking a lively and intelligent interest in Teddy's experiments.

Every one knows that in the early part of 1894, Pondoland, the last independent native State south of Natal, was annexed to Cape Colony. Much to the general surprise, the annexation was effected peacefully, but for some months afterwards the greatest care had to be exercised in dealing with the Pondos. The people generally were glad of the change from the harsh, arbitrary, and irresponsible rule of the native chiefs to the settled and equitable conditions of civilised government; but the chiefs gave trouble. They naturally would not, without struggling and agitating, submit to the loss of power and prestige which they sustained, and they bitterly resented being no longer permitted to "eat up" those who annoyed them. Now, the instincts of clannishness and loyalty are so strong amongst the Kafirs, that even against what they well know to be their own vital interests, they will follow the most cruel and rapacious tyrant, so long as he is their hereditary tribal chieftain, into rebellion.

Now, the Kwesa clan of Pondos dwelt just on the boundary of Mount Loch, and within thirty miles of the Magistracy. The head of this clan, a chief named Sololo, had not objected to the annexation, and was consequently looked upon as well-affected towards the Government. But within a few months after the annexation, a serious difficulty arose between the authorities and this man. One of his followers quarrelled with another, and after the time-honoured local custom, assuaged his feelings by means of a spear-thrust, which had a fatal result. The murdered man was one whom Sololo disliked, whereas, on the other hand, the murderer was one whom the chief delighted to honour. Consequently, when the magistrate demanded the surrender of the culprit for the purpose of dealing with him according to law, Sololo refused delivery, and couched his refusal in an extremely insolent and rebellious message.

Cajolements, remonstrances, and threats were of no avail; Sololo remained obstinate. His tone, however, somewhat changed; he sent polite, but evasive and unsatisfactory replies to all messages on the subject. The Chief Magistrate was at his wits' end. Of course the law had to be vindicated, but were an armed force to be sent against Sololo, the odds were ten to one that within twenty-four hours signal fires would be blazing on every hill, and the war-cry sounding from one end of Pondoland to the other. The Chief Magistrate's native name was "Indabeni, " which means "The one of counsel. " He was a man of vast experience in respect of the natives, and moreover, he did not belong to that highly moral, but sometimes inconvenient class of officials who are known as "the hide-bound"; that is to say, his ideas ranged beyond the length of the longest piece of red tape in his office, and he knew for a certainty that things existed which could not conveniently be wrapped up in foolscap paper. He was, moreover, one who trusted much to the effect of his own considerable personal influence, and he believed in utilising the talents of such of his subordinates as possessed faculties similar to his own in this respect.

Indabeni had taken Vooda's measure accurately. He knew the Constable to have a persuasive tongue, to be honest, loyal, and discreet, and, above all, to possess that nameless and almost indescribable quality of imparting trustfulness in those with whom he came in contact.

One afternoon a telegram marked "confidential" came from Indabeni to the Resident Magistrate of Mount Loch. The purport of the message was that Vooda should go to Sololo and talk quietly to him, endeavouring by means of persuasion to effect a compliance with the reasonable demands of Government. Teddy, being in the fullest confidence of his Chief, was present when instructions were accordingly given to Vooda, who was directed to start early next morning for the kraal of the Chief of the Kwesas, in Pondoland.

When the offices were closed for the day, Teddy went home to his hut, and it was noticed by one who met him on the road that his manner was very preoccupied, and his walk unusually slow. Shortly afterwards he was seen to stroll over to the police camp, and go straight to Vooda's hut.

At eight o'clock that evening Vooda visited Teddy's dwelling, and a long and serious conversation ensued. This was varied by a series of experiments of a nature so striking that even Vooda was startled. At about ten o'clock a stranger passing noticed strange flashes lighting up the back of the hut behind the reed fence. Shortly before eleven Vooda returned to camp, carrying a small satchel which contained a packet of lycopodium powder, a piece of potassium about as large as a walnut, and a number of whitish lumps about an inch in diameter, such as are known amongst practitioners of parlour magic variously as "serpents' eggs" or "Pharaoh's serpents. "

At daylight next morning Vooda left the police camp, but it was late in the afternoon when he reached the kraal of Sololo. He found a. number of strangers there, including Shasha, the "inyanga, " or war doctor. The men, all of whom were armed, were sitting on the ground in a half-circle. Before them stood a number of large earthen pots of beer. Vooda, being an old friend of the Chief, was invited to sit down and drink, so, after removing the saddle from his horse, he joined the party. He soon saw, however, that his presence had imported an element of restraint. He was careful as yet not to allude to the business upon which he had come. Later on others began to arrive, some carrying guns, some spears, and some assegais. It was plain that an important discussion was on hand, and that Vooda's presence was unwelcome. The beer was not in sufficient quantities to cause intoxication, but nevertheless all were somewhat mellow when the sun went down.

Shortly afterwards Sololo asked the visitor point blank "Where he was thinking of. " This was an unusual thing to do under the circumstances, such a question to a visitor being held amongst natives to be discourteous and suggestive of inhospitality.

Vooda replied to the effect that he had an important matter to discuss with the Chief, and asked Sololo to grant him a private interview.

Now Sololo, having had experience of Vooda's persuasive tongue and knack of casuistry, did not wish to argue the point—knowing, as he did full well, the object of Vooda's visit—and at once made up his mind that he would not see the glib-tongued constable alone.

"Son of my father, " he said, "what you have to say, let it be said before these my councilors and friends. "

Vooda saw there was no chance of a private discussion, and determined therefore to play his game boldly and in public. The dusk of evening was just setting in, and some women had kindled a bright fire.

"My Chief, " he said, "I come with the words of Indabeni, who has chosen me because he knows I am your younger brother" (figurative).

"Indabeni is a great man, " said Sololo; "he has eyes all round his head. His words are good to hear—speak them, son of my father. "

"Indabeni's heart is heavy, my Chief, because you, the leopard, are placing yourself in the path of the buffalo, which is the Government. Men have told Indabeni that you refuse to deliver to the Magistrate one who has done wrong. "

"The leopard may stand on one side and tear the flank of the buffalo as he passes. He may then hide in the caves of the rocks where the buffalo cannot follow, " said Sololo, sententiously.

"The buffalo may call the wolves to his aid to drive the leopard from his cave, " rejoined Vooda, developing the allegory further; "but why will you not give up the wrong-doer to the magistrate? "

"Why must I give up my friend to be choked with a rope? " said Sololo, excitedly. "He has not slain a white man, but one of my own people. Government must leave him to be punished according to the law of the native. If one of my tribe slays a white man, I will deliver up the slayer. "

"But you know what the Government is, my Chief—it is over all of us. Even Indabeni himself has to do as it tells him. "

"Indabeni is not a Pondo, neither am I Indabeni," said Sololo, appealing, with a look, to the audience.

"Yebo, Yebo, Ewe—E-hea," shouted all the men.

"I did not ask Government for its laws," continued the Chief. "'U-Sessellodes' [The native attempt at pronouncing the name of Mr. Cecil Rhodes, Premier of the Cape Colony.] came here and said in a loud voice that we all belonged to him. We were surprised, and could not think or speak. Besides, who listens to the bleating of a goat when an angry bull bellows? Now we have thought and spoken together, and we can also fight; I will never give up my friend to be choked with a rope."

"E-hea," shouted the audience.

"My Chief," said Vooda, "your words are like milk flowing from a great black cow ten days after she has calved, but there is one thing you have not seen, but which I have seen and trembled at."

"What is this thing that frightens a man who is the father of children?"

"The magic (umtagati) of U-Sessellodes, which he has taught to Indabeni—the terrible magic wherewith he overthrew Lo Bengula and the Matabele."

"We, also, have our magic," said Sololo, glancing at Shasha, the war-doctor.

Shasha came forward in a half-crouching attitude, and approached Vooda, who appeared to be very much impressed. The war-doctor's appearance was startling enough. He was an elderly man of hideous aspect. On his head he wore a high cap of baboon skin. Slung around his neck, waist, elbows, wrists, knees, and ankles were all sorts of extraordinary things—cowrie and tortoise-shells, teeth and claws of various beasts of prey, strips of skin from all kinds of animals, inflated gall bladders, bones, and pieces of wood. In his hand he carried a bag made by cutting the skin of a wild cat around the neck, and then tearing it off the body as one skins an eel. Out of this he drew a long, living, green snake (inusbwa, the boom-slang), which he hung over his shoulder, where it began to coil about, darting out its forked tongue.

As Shasha advanced quivering towards Vooda in short, abrupt springs, all the things hanging about him clashed and rattled together. He bent down and beat the ground with the palms of his hands and the soles of his feet, making the while a low rumbling in his throat, the apple of which worked up and down. His eyes glared and his nostrils dilated. The snake hissed, and wound itself round his neck and limbs. The whole audience appeared to be struck with superstitious dread.

Shasha suddenly drew himself straight up, and chanted in a sing-song voice, rattling his charms at every period:

"I am the ruler of the baboons and the master of the owls. I talk to the wild cat in the hush. I call Tikoloshe (a water spirit) out of the river in the night-time and ask him questions. I make sickness do my bidding on men and cattle. I drive it away when I like. I can bring blight to the crops, and stop the milk of cows. I can, by my magic medicines, find out the wicked ones who do these things. I alone can look upon Icanti (a fabulous serpent) and not die. I know the mountain where Impandulu (the Lightning Bird) builds its nest. I can make men invulnerable in battle with my medicines, and I can cause the enemies of my Chief to run like a bush-buck pursued by dogs."

The speech ended, Shasha again bowed down, quivering and contorting, beat the ground with his hands and the soles of his feet and then sprang aside into the darkness.

Sololo looked at Vooda as though he would say, "What do you think of that; is he not a most terribly potent war-doctor?" All the other men looked extremely terrified.

Dead silence reigned for a few moments, and then Vooda spoke:

"O Chief, the magic of your war-doctor is indeed dreadful to behold, but, believe me, the magic of U-Sessellodes and Indabeni is stronger, and I can prove it."

This caused a murmur of incredulity and indignation. The magic paraphernalia of the war-doctor rattled ominously in the gloom.

"U-Sessellodes," continued Vooda, "has found the Lightning Bird sitting upon its nest, and plucked its feathers; he has discovered how to make water burn, and he has robbed the cave of Icanti of its eggs, which he can strew over the land to hatch in the sun, and produce snakes that will kill all who see them. These secrets he has taught to Indabeni, and Indabeni has taught them to me so that I might warn you, and having warned, prove the truth of my words. "

At this a loud "ho, ho, " accompanied by a rattling noise, was heard from the war-doctor. Sololo laughed sarcastically. Several of the audience did the same. Then Sololo said:

"Are we children, to believe these things? "

"My Chief, " said Vooda, impressively, "you are not a child, neither is Indabeni; as you know, —nor is the potent war-doctor, nor are any of these great men (madoda roakulu) that I see around me. For that matter, neither am I a child. I have said that I can prove my words, and I say so again. "

"Prove them, then, " said Sololo.

"Three things will I do to show the magic of U-Sessellodes, which he has taught to Indabeni—I will show you a feather of the Lightning Bird, I will make water burn like dry wood, and I will produce some of the eggs of Icanti and make them, when touched with fire, hatch into young serpents before your eyes. "

There was not a breath of wind. Vooda seized a small firebrand, and stepped a few yards away from the fire. He held the firebrand in his left hand, and put his right into one of the pockets of his tunic. This pocket contained a quantity of loose lycopodium powder. He filled his hand with this, waved it over his head several times, and then projected the handful of powder high into the air with a sweeping throw. Then he slowly lifted the firebrand, and as the cloud of powder descended, it ignited with a silent, blinding flash. A loud "Mawo" from the spectators greeted the success of the experiment.

The war-doctor gave a harsh laugh and shouted that there was no magic in the business, and that the Lightning Bird's plumage was still intact so far as Vooda was concerned; he, the war-doctor, knew how the thing was done, and would presently explain. Sololo and the others murmured amongst themselves.

"Now, " said Vooda, "I will make water burn with a bright flame like dry wood. "

"You have, no doubt, brought the water with you in a bottle, " said Shasha, the war-doctor, with a sneer in his voice. He was evidently thinking of paraffin.

"No, O most potent controller of baboons, " said Vooda, "I will, on the contrary, ask you to get me some water for the purpose, in a vessel of your own choice. "

Shasha went to one of the huts and returned with a small earthen pot full of water, which he placed on the ground near the fire.

Vooda look the lump of potassium which he had cut into the form of a large conical bullet, from his pocket, and advanced to where the chief was sitting. He beckoned to the war-doctor to approach, and then, said:

"This, O chief, and O discourser-with-the-wild-cat, is a new and wonderful kind of lead which U-Sessellodes has dug out of a hole in the ground far deeper than any other hole that was ever made. You will observe that my knife is sharp, and therefore I cut the lead easily. You may see how the metal shines when newly cut. Now, if a bullet such as this be shot into a river, the water blazes up and consumes the land. "

"Give it to me that I may examine it, " said Shasha.

Vooda handed a small paring of the potassium to the war-doctor, saying;

"Be very careful, O you-whom-the-owls-obey-in-the-dark, because it is dangerous stuff. "

Shasha did exactly what Vooda anticipated — he looked carefully at the shred of metal, and lifted it to his mouth, meaning to test it with his teeth. When, however, the potassium touched the saliva, it blazed up, and the unhappy war-doctor spat it out with a fearful yell. His lips and tongue were severely burnt. Sololo and the men, who had seen the flame issuing from Shasha's mouth, were terror-stricken.

Vooda now cut the lump of potassium into several pieces, and these he dropped into the pot of water. The lumps began to flame brilliantly, dancing on the top of the water and gyrating across and around. All the spectators were horribly frightened, and shrank back, their eyeballs starting, and their lips wide apart.

"Now, " said Vooda, who felt that he had practically won the game, "I will produce the eggs of Icanti, the terrible serpent, and make them hatch out live snakes. Were I to do this without having other greater magic ready wherewith to overcome them, the snakes would kill us all. The only magic stronger than that of Icanti is the magic of the Lightning Bird, so I will drop a feather plucked by U-Sessellodes from the tail of Impandulu upon the snakes as they come out of the eggs, and that will cause them to turn into dust. "

Vooda took five large Pharaoh's serpent-eggs out of his pocket and placed them on a flat stone about a yard from the fire. He then asked Shasha to approach, warning him to be very careful, as the serpents might be dangerous. After the experience with the potassium, such a warning to Shasha was quite a work of supererogation. He came forward with hesitating steps, and stood behind Vooda, watching.

Vooda had a small quantity of lycopodium powder in his left hand. With his right he seized a blazing firebrand, and with this he touched each of the eggs in turn. At once five horrible looking snakes began uncoiling, blue flame surrounding the spot at which each emerged from its egg. Vooda then shouted loudly, calling on the name of Impandulu, and making mystic passes over the coiling horror with his fire-brand. Stretching forth his left hand, he liberated a small cloud of lycopodium powder, which ignited with a brilliant flash. At this, all the spectators leaped to their feet, wildly yelling, and, with the exception of Sololo, who stood still—although the picture of terror— disappeared into the surrounding darkness. For some seconds after the sound of the last footfall had died away, the rattle of Shasha's charms, as he fled, could be heard.

Vooda approached Sololo:

"My Chief, what word am I to carry to Indabeni? "

"Tell Indabeni that the wrong-doer will be given up to the Magistrate to choke with a rope. Yet you need not tell him, because the man will be in the Magistrate's hand before your voice can reach Indabeni's ear."

And so he was.

Thus was a war averted, and yet neither Vooda nor Teddy Morton ever received any reward for their distinguished services.

THE END